I0825455

THE DAILY CONNOISSEUR'S GUIDE TO

Living Well at Home

THE DAILY CONNOISSEUR'S GUIDE TO
Living Well at Home

Making Everyday Life Extraordinary

JENNIFER L. SCOTT

Illustrated by Alice Tait

83 Press
2323 2nd Avenue North
Birmingham, AL 35203
83press.com

For information about special discounts for bulk purchases, please contact 83 Press Special Sales at 205-995-8860 or customerservice@hoffmanmedia.com

ISBN #979-8-9923852-8-1
ISBN #979-8-9923852-9-8 (e-book)
Printed in USA

For Leslie and Jason,
who keep a beautiful home

"The home should be the treasure chest of living."

—LE CORBUSIER

Contents

PART II: BEAUTY

PART III: INSPIRATION

CONCLUSION

Introduction

THE CONSCIOUSNESS OF HOME

"Anne and Diana found the drive home as pleasant as the drive in—pleasanter, indeed, since there was the delightful consciousness of home waiting at the end of it."

—LUCY MAUD MONTGOMERY,
ANNE OF GREEN GABLES

I love my life at home. Truly. There is no place I would rather be. And when I am away for too long a period, I long for my space: our humble abode, decorated to our tastes and effectively run to meet our needs. My homelife hasn't always been idyllic, and it still isn't perfect. It's taken me nearly two decades to even arrive at this point, and there is much more to my journey ahead, but my skills in homemaking have come a long way. I used to run my home inefficiently: overcome by clutter and run on "survival mode" cleaning routines. And as for aesthetics? For years upon years, our space was only

partially decorated to our tastes. We were always holding off decorating and making improvements because we said whatever home we were living in wasn't our "forever home," and we needed to keep it neutral for resale value. The result of all this was desultory living. It's like I was longing to live an excellent life at home but at the same time imposing limitations that were unknowingly holding me back from this dream. Thankfully, with trial, error, lots of introspection, and experimentation, I have become more intentional about how I live while there, and thus, daily life is a joyful adventure, one that gladly takes me to my cozy, well-fitted bed every evening.

I grew up in the suburbs of Los Angeles, California, in a small house with my mom, dad, and sister. Our house was not grand or fancy, but it was a haven for me. Surrounded by my dad's extensive book collection and my mother's enchanting garden, I cultivated a love of home from a very young age—one that exalted the joy of domestic leisure. My appreciation for beautiful living was magnified as I grew older and was exposed to different cultures and other ways of life. Notably, when I was a junior in college, I studied abroad and lived with a Parisian family. Their beautiful way of living inspired me tremendously and was the impetus for my first book, *Lessons from Madame Chic*, and the rest of the Madame Chic series. But France and my childhood home are not the only inspirations I draw on for excellent daily living. As you'll see later in the book, inspiration can be found everywhere and in the most unexpected ways.

The Daily Connoisseur's Guide to Living Well at Home shares the key lessons I've learned on beautiful living. Part I, Function, implements helpful routines to run a home efficiently through the two-fold system of method and order. Part II, Beauty, shares how we can make our homelife not only comfortable but beautiful and extols the simple pleasures of fine living on a budget. And Part III, Inspiration, shares the wisdom I've gleaned from well-run establishments I've visited around the world to bring the best of domestic living to you.

Think of the most wonderful days in your home: when you dine well, your space is tidy, and your eyes are pleased by what you see. These days do not need to be one-off occurrences. These experiences can be your everyday reality, and even if they're not, guess what? You're still going to enjoy your life anyway because we are not only working on our outer circumstances but our inner mindset as well.

Regardless of what ends up being your "forever home," a key tenet of *The Daily Connoisseur* strategy is to live well now in the home you currently live in. The advice holds for various similar circumstances. For example, if someone is trying to lose or gain weight, the advice from the style experts is: don't hold off on dressing well until you get to that ideal weight. *Dress well now*. If you are driving a car you don't like, keep it clean and running optimally and appreciate it as it is *now* while you have it. You still strive for your ideals, but you don't put your life on hold waiting for them to happen. You begin to live well *now* as if you are currently living your dream. Even if you're renting a small apartment but dream about owning a home in the country, don't hold off on decorating, organizing, and living well in your current space. Living well brings joy, creativity, and vitality to your life—three things that can only benefit you and bring you closer to your goals. Before you know it, you might find yourself in your country home thinking fondly of those days in the studio apartment.

Much of our success in life is determined by how we live at home in our private world. If it is a cluttered mess, not decorated to our tastes and not running efficiently, homelife can be frustrating. This can lead to a strong desire to leave the home—to constantly eat out and seek excitement elsewhere. But when attention is put on the home, in living well and beautifully, the excitement is found within your four walls. No greater feeling exists. Making sure you get your homelife "right" is worth all the time and effort it will take you. Just like exercise, eating healthful meals, and grooming yourself will make your body feel and look good; we must put the same effort into our life at home. When it is running efficiently, like a small boutique hotel decorated to our tastes and cozy as can be, home becomes a much-needed sanctuary from the outside world.

At the beginning of this introduction, I shared a quote from *Anne of Green Gables* on the consciousness of home that I have thought about often over the years. Our homes are physical dwellings that provide shelter on the most basic level—a refuge from the natural elements. On a deeper level, they have a consciousness, one that we all tap into whether we realize it or not. The consciousness is hard to define, but some of its attributes involve the scents, memories, feelings, and emotions associated with home. It is these elements that tug at our heartstrings and beckon us back with anticipation when we are away for too long. While the elements of consciousness are hard to define, there are definite techniques to optimize their potency.

Throughout the book are several journaling prompts that will aid you on the way. I highly encourage you to follow the prompts and record this experience. In fact, it might be a good idea to allot a dedicated notebook to this process so you can keep all your home-related ideas and progress-tracking in one place. Writing down your strategies and observations will only enhance your endeavors.

So let us develop this delightful consciousness of home here and now by going on this adventure together. On this first-class journey, we will establish and prioritize method, order, comfort, and beauty to become true connoisseurs of daily life. Let's begin, shall we? ❖

PART I:
FUNCTION

Method & Order

"Hercule Poirot's methods are his own. Order and method and "the little grey cells."
—AGATHA CHRISTIE, *THE BIG FOUR*

When we become conscious of our homelife and how we wish to improve it, miracles begin to occur. Conscious attention will bring forth the areas in which our homes need our love and attention. If there is any part of your day that is persistently a problem, for example, you find yourself not eating healthful meals because of lack of preparation, or you consistently can't find important papers, becoming conscious of these struggles is the first step to solving them. People can go years without addressing the basic issues of living well at home, becoming accustomed to disorder and faulty living. The opposite of consciousness is unconsciousness in the same way being unthoughtful is the opposite of thoughtfulness. When someone is not thoughtful, they do things without consideration by "going through the motions," usually to disastrous results. If unconsciousness continues as with the prior examples, the food budget is exceeded each month because there is "nothing to eat" at home, resulting in more meals out or important deadlines left unmet because the papers were lost. When cultivating a home of consciousness, we want elevated thought and intention behind everything we do. In turn, these problems will be solved, and a delightful way of living established.

> **"The key to growth is the introduction of higher dimensions of consciousness into our awareness."**
>
> —LAO TZU

Lao Tzu describes growth as introducing higher dimensions of consciousness to our awareness. With every problem in our home, we must explore the higher dimension of what we desire. If we are spending too much money on takeout and not eating healthy, we must focus on the bigger picture. What are we striving for? How do we want to see growth in this area? We would like healthful meals on a regular basis to nourish the whole family while staying within budget and enjoying the process of not only creating the meals but eating them, too.

Once these elevated desires have been acknowledged, the way has been made for their thoughtful implementation to be carried out. When you write down the intentions and plans, action is set in motion and ready to follow through. Old unconscious habits are broken, and new, higher dimensional habits are formed.

To build up the consciousness of our home, the one Anne of Green Gables so longed for, we are going to be thoughtful about every aspect of homelife. We will not only put systems in place for running our homes but actually use the systems, too. We will clarify how we want to eat and create meal plans for ultimate success. We will set up cleaning routines that are easy to implement and follow through on, so our homes operate on cleanliness. We will decorate according to our true style, and the result of these plans and actions will be that our abode becomes a conscious hub of wonderful activity for resting, entertaining, creating, and nourishing. Let's begin with implementing the systems. Because without a proper plan, nothing can get done.

If aiming to live well at home, we must have an organized homelife that supports our everyday aspirations. Method and order are the critical foundations that run each home. This is the impetus of getting organized. Organization doesn't come easily for most people, but a sense of method and order is the first layer that must be laid down to have a pleasant life at home. Certainly, styling your fireplace mantel and choosing wallpaper for your bedroom are much more enjoyable than coming up with a system to file your office papers, but a system must be created, or the stress from the unfiled papers will not allow you to appreciate your cozy hearth or patterned wallpaper.

Think of home organization like you would your physical health. You can put on a beautiful dress, apply lipstick, and spritz perfume (decorate the home), but if your health is poor, it's hard to get through your day. Certainly, looking good helps, but getting your health back to optimal levels is what should be focused on. In this sense, the health of our home is gauged through method and order and the functioning systems we rely on every day.

WHERE DID YOUR HABITS COME FROM?

If you have disorderly habits, you likely learned them as a child and carried them into adulthood. I have found it helpful to think of my own personal history with orderliness and organization to correct my bad habits. Think of how you were taught to tidy as a child. Did your parents require you to clean your room? Was it a task that you liked or were you always trying to get out of doing it? Were you only required to clean your room when you got in trouble or was it an everyday requirement? Did you have a parent who cleaned your room for you, so you never had to do too much? Or were you required to be so neat as a child, you vowed that when you became an adult, you wouldn't be so uptight about your living space? Often, the habits we form in childhood are not based on pleasure and joy but on requirement. Unless the positive principles of tidiness and organization were taught and ingrained at an early age, you likely struggled to build those habits as an adult.

Journaling Prompt:

What was your childhood experience like with tidiness and organization? How did you feel about keeping your room clean as a child? Were you overwhelmed by the process, or did you enjoy keeping a tidy space? How did you tidy your room when you were younger? Did you help in other areas of the home? If so, where? How did you feel about this?

Here is my story: I loved my childhood bedroom. My parents let me decorate it to my exact tastes. I had frilly floral bedding and spring green walls. My favorite Victorian dolls and all their accoutrements were displayed on my dresser. Even though I had a pretty room, it would often get messy after long sessions of playing with my toys. I would emerge from these imaginative sessions with doll clothes, accessories, books, and miscellany scattered everywhere. My parents would ask me to clean my room, but I didn't know how to begin. Where should I start first? Putting the doll clothes away? What about my own clothes? How did those get mixed up on the floor, too? What about all the scattered doll furniture? I didn't have time to put it back in the dollhouse properly, so I just shoved it under my bed for when I could do it "correctly." The mess was so big; I felt overwhelmed and didn't know where to start. This resulted in me whining and getting in trouble. I took that feeling of overwhelmingness with me as an adult. When I moved out of my childhood home and went to live with college roommates and then eventually got married and established my own home, I was able to keep it together by keeping my space relatively tidy, but there were no systems of organization in place. That same "shove-it-under-the-bed" mentality still plagued me as an adult. As I journaled about my history with tidiness, I realized I needed to establish systems to combat my feelings of being overwhelmed and see results. Instead of looking at the mess on the floor of my room as one giant blob that I wanted to push under the bed, I could have created a space to house each category of toy I was playing with and calmly and methodically put them back when I was finished.

British educator Charlotte Mason likened habit development to "laying down rails." Much like a railroad track lays down rails for the train to travel on, everything we do in life lays down rails of habits, whether good or bad. Our goal for excellent homemaking is to lay down the rails of great habits. This will require intention, consciousness, patience, and follow-through. We lay down the rails for method and order in the home by implementing systems and steadily sticking to them . . . *no matter what.*

In *Mrs. Beeton's Book of Household Management*, Mrs. Beeton writes, *"Order, again, is indispensable; for by it we wish to be understood that 'there should be a place for everything, and everything in its place.' Method, too, is most necessary; for when the work is properly contrived and each part arranged in regular succession, it will be done more quickly and more effectually."* In short, method and order are about establishing a system and adhering to it.

METHOD

Method is the plan, the solution, and the conscious decision. It should be thought through, written down on paper, and discussed and implemented with the people you live with. Where do you even begin with establishing your method? The best way to answer this question is to look to your home itself. Your home will dictate to you what needs to be done.

> **"The daily duties of a housekeeper are regulated, in a great measure, by the extent of the establishment she superintends."**
>
> —MRS. BEETON

Keeping this in mind, we will create a bespoke organizational system to implement your new positive methods. Savor the journey knowing that you are making changes to your life that will improve your home in countless ways.

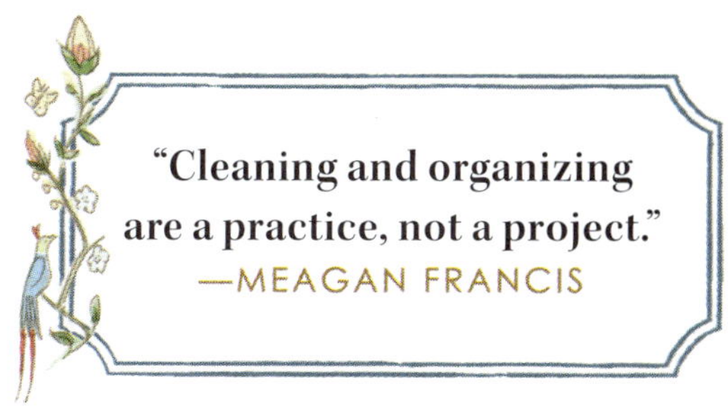

ORDER

If method is the plan, order is the action. This is the follow-through of the plan. Think of the Constitution of the United States of America. Our Founding Fathers wrote the Constitution (method) down on paper and signed it. Then, the Constitution became the law of the land, and citizens are to follow it (order). Once you write down your method, you will actively enact the plan as if it were the law of the land. This might sound limiting, but my experience has shown that rules can actually be liberating. We will free ourselves from chaos by establishing order. Method and order must go together. You cannot have one without the other. There is no point having a law (method) if no one obeys it (order).

Let's say that your method for dealing with incoming mail is to immediately recycle junk mail and then place the important letters in the file folder in your command center to be dealt with every Tuesday at 4:00 p.m. That's a great method! It's clear and concise. It has easy steps to follow. It can easily be shared with everyone in the family, and the follow-through set forth is practical. You implement this method for the mail. But then you go check the mail and forget to immediately sort through it. So, you lay it on the dining room table where it sits for three days. Then, the children put their schoolwork on top of it, and it becomes a larger pile that gets moved to a kitchen counter when the dining table is needed. In the back of your mind, you know the mail is there somewhere and that you really should go through it. What was the day you set aside for that? Oh well, you'll get to it later this afternoon. But the afternoon gets busy and then you forget. A few days later, that pile has migrated to the top of the armoire in the hallway, with the hope that it will be sorted out later. A few more days pass, and you decide to do some housework, so you take down the pile and put everything where it belongs. You come across the important mail and realize that two of the bills were due three days ago. You rush to your computer to pay them online. The pile of half-opened mail sits on the kitchen table now along with the homework that needed to be put away. In this scenario, the method was established, but the order was not carried out, so the operation was rendered useless.

Here is how it would ideally look. You set your method in place and write it down in your planner or journal. You check the mail on your way home from running errands. As soon as you step in the door, the dog jumps on you wanting to go out and the kids are asking for a snack. You calmly place your handbag in the hallway cubby and sort through the mail in your hand to determine what is important and what isn't. You received some advertisements, a few bills, and a letter from a friend. You recycle the unneeded mail and place the three important bills in your command center file. You bring the letter upstairs to your writing desk to read when you have a quiet moment. The whole process took less than one minute. When Tuesday rolls around, head to the command center to pay the bills and reply to the letter. You remember to do this because you wrote it down in your planner. (For recurring events, you can set a reminder on your phone.) This step took less than 15 minutes of your time. You file the paperwork where it belongs and move on with your day.

The second example shows the calm assuredness that method and order bring to life. Yes, it is predictable and staid, but that is what you are going for. You are going for strictly adhered to practices that become a natural part of your daily and weekly routine. This creates an actual air of order in the home, which is dictated by the unseen method. The first example displays nothing but chaos, which leads to late fees and a slowly migrating mess that plagues your home with disorder. The second example gets the bills paid on time and filed away with the least chaos possible. Clearly method and order (example number two) are what we are aiming for to create a peaceful, harmonious, and orderly life at home.

> **"Edit your life frequently and ruthlessly. It's your masterpiece after all."**
> —NATHAN W. MORRIS

Bespoke Organization 

"Good order is the foundation of all great things."
—EDMUND BURKE

The next step to getting organized is to create a bespoke organizational system with a foundation of method and order that addresses the needs of your home. Getting organized once and for all isn't as daunting as it might sound. This system will be easy to create as the problem areas are generally obvious. Let your home guide you here. Be attuned to any area where there is dissatisfaction and proceed from there. To use a prior example, if you find that you are spending too much money on takeout food and restaurant dining and would like to dine at home more, you can create a bespoke system for meal planning, grocery shopping, and weekly meal preparation. Remember, the first step is to become aware of the dissatisfaction. When you notice your monthly expenditure and are unhappy with the large amount spent on meals, this unease should be the catalyst for change.

We become aware of our pain points at home much like we do with our own bodies. If you are going about your day and notice a painful twinge in your lower back, for example, you pause and notice it. You wonder why it's there. You look back on the day and ask yourself what you could have done to possibly injure your back. Because the pain is there, it needs to be addressed, so you might take a painkiller and book an appointment with your doctor. You don't go on living with the pain, ignoring it, and just trying to get on with your day. When you have bodily pain, you likely address it immediately and try to get rid of it as soon as possible. For some reason, we don't do this with our homelife. When we identify a pain point at home, often we ignore it and hope it just goes away. But it rarely does because all problems must be solved with consciousness and attention. Ignoring them will get us nowhere. Knowing this, we will take the same steps when creating our organizational systems. Where are the pain points? Then, the method (solution) can be established by thinking about it and thus creating it, refining it, and writing it down. Next, the order can be implemented by carrying it out. When you carry out the order, be fully aware of its progress. Do you feel this is a beneficial system? Is it practical? Is it enjoyable? Will it work long-term? Make tweaks to your system, if necessary. Keep it as a living document, not one that is set in stone. The most important aspect of this is to enjoy the process.

Many people think of organization, creating new habits and systems and other foundational practices, as being unpleasant. But focus on the positive news that you are actively working to improve your homelife for the better. Encourage yourself by affirming that not only will the end results be satisfying but the journey will be an adventure. You are bringing consciousness to your home, and the movement from this shift should energize you.

I find that the best way to journal this is by identifying the issue and writing down how you ideally want to live. Focus on affirmations, rather than negative observations, when you journal. For instance, with the previous meal planning example, the affirmation should be:

"I cook healthful meals at home and stay on budget every month."

Writing the ideal is more encouraging than focusing on the current negative situation. If you wrote, "I am tired of going over budget on food each month and eating too much takeout," that expression focuses more on the problem and does not offer a solution. When we focus on the positive solution, we can move forward with assurance and hope. Here are a few more examples:

Problem: Bills are often forgotten and not paid on time. Important correspondence goes missing.

Instead of writing: The bills always go missing and are never paid on time; we need to fix this.

Write this instead:

Method *(positive affirmation)*: Bills are kept in the same place and paid in a timely manner, twice a month, then filed away when paid.

The negative observation shows the old way. We will not look back, and that will not be our way anymore. By focusing on the positive affirmation, you can feel hope that a positive change is coming. Now, we will write the order so it can be implemented.

Order *(positive affirmation)*: Once collected, junk mail is recycled, and important bills and correspondence immediately go in the command center. The bills are paid on the second Tuesday of every month. Once paid, the bills are filed away in the monthly file.

Knowing these techniques, you can now create a bespoke organizational system that will fit your needs perfectly by allowing the establishment of your home to dictate the need. Make a cup of tea and sit down with a good pencil and write down your plan. The great news is that you only need to focus on the troublesome areas here. If you already have systems that are working well for you, leave those alone. *If it's not broken, don't fix it.* But in your bespoke organizational system, you will continue with what is working and only fix the problems.

Think about how your home runs and write down the areas of concern starting with the biggest snags in your organizational system. Is the laundry perpetually piled on the sofa waiting to be folded? Are the bills scattered around the kitchen countertops? Are your bathroom drawers jammed with old, expired products, requiring your everyday products to sit cluttered on your countertop? Think of the biggest grievances you have with running the system of your home.

Let's take the example of the laundry on the sofa. Yes, we are going to have it folded and put away, but that is not going to solve the organization problem. *A system needs to be put in place so that it doesn't regularly happen again.* This system needs to be written down, discussed with the family, and adhered to . . . strictly. In your journal, write down the family solution, which will likely be a schedule for what gets washed when and who is taking care of it from start to finish. If needed, laundry baskets will be placed in strategic locations, and the cupboard of the laundry room will be restocked to make laundering a breeze.

The second example involves bills being scattered across the kitchen countertops. Yes, the bills can be paid now, but going forward, you need a plan to end the cycle of disorganization. Write down "command center" and designate a place where this will be. Whenever you walk into your home with the mail, you will go directly there to drop the mail off. This will be in a location you regularly see (not hidden away, or you might forget to pay the bills—yikes!), and the whole family knows that this is where the important mail is stored. You are implementing solutions and action, method and order.

The final example references crammed bathroom drawers. Yes, you can go right now and declutter them, but how are you going to prevent these drawers from getting cluttered again in six months? Perhaps you can sort through the drawers every month to ensure you are not storing expired products that need to be thrown out or harboring beauty items you don't actually use. (We explore the cluttered bathroom countertops further in the next section.) It's time to write down your action plan.

Most common areas in the home that require a plan of method and order:

The Entryway
The Mail
The Wardrobe
The Laundry
The Clutter Hot Spots

Sample plans for problem areas:

Problem: The entryway becomes cluttered with shoes, handbags, coats, and other miscellaneous items, choking the entry to the home.

Solution: Family members regularly go through their belongings stored in the entryway. Out-of-season shoes and outerwear are stored away in a spare closet. Only the most current shoes, handbag, and accessories are stored in the entry hallway. A regular assessment takes place on the first of every month and is scheduled in the planner.

Problem: The kitchen counter gets cluttered with homework, miscellaneous objects, books, and flyers.

Solution: During the nightly kitchen tidy, the countertops are also cleared of clutter. Homework goes back in backpacks, books put away, and flyers recycled.

Problem: Bathroom countertops are cluttered with too many products.

Solution: Bathroom drawers are cleaned out every two months (scheduled in the planner). Expired or empty products are thrown away, drawers are wiped down, and countertop products that are still used are placed in the drawers for easy access.

Problem: Children's drawers are bursting with clothes. They are running out of storage.

Solution: Every three months, the children go through their clothes, placing all garments that no longer fit into a donation bag. All clothing that remains is placed neatly back in drawers and hung in the closet.

GET SPECIFIC

Let's zoom in on how we can make these bespoke organizational systems work for us. How does one acquire a knack for organization when they weren't born with one? Most people are not born with a talent for organization. (I most certainly was not.) Habits are created when you perform the same action or behavior repeatedly. Most of our organizational and tidiness habits are formed in childhood. If we desire to change these habits, a specific formula of awareness + conscious regular practice (of the new habit) must take place. Awareness of the problem itself must first occur for you to consciously practice the new habit and make that your new reality.

AWARENESS + Conscious Regular Practice
= Good Habit Formation

Let's explore the cluttered bathroom countertop example here. If you struggle with putting things back in their rightful place, the first step is to acknowledge this (awareness). But don't shame yourself with this problem. We will focus on the solution. Using the affirmation technique, write a statement in your journal that goes something like this:

"I easily put my belongings back where they belong. This is the new me."

Repeat this affirmation silently or verbally as often as you need until it becomes who you are. In other words, fake it until you make it. This will let your subconscious know that you are ready to change your bad habit into a positive one.

Once you have consciously acknowledged this problem and focused on the new habit you'd like to establish, it helps to get even more specific. This is venturing deeper into awareness. Which belongings do you have trouble putting back? Your makeup? Skin care items? All the above? Once you identify what you struggle to put back, ask yourself "why?" and employ your powers of observation.

If you struggle to put your makeup and skin care items away after you use them, for example, observe the products strewn across your countertop, making the bathroom appear messy. You know they should go back in your drawer, but then you open your drawer and notice it is already full of other products. Taking note of what is going on precisely will help you implement the method for taking care of this problem. Because your drawers are full of unused and expired products, you will need to go through and clear those out. Then, any organizational details you can add that will aid you in putting your makeup and skin care items back easily, like dividers, will only help the process. Clean out the drawers with a damp cloth. Line them with wallpaper scraps or with a pretty drawer liner (this will make the drawers visually pleasing and make you *want* to open them up every day), then place the new dividers inside. Place the makeup and skin care items in according to how you use them and how easily you can reach them in the drawer, with the most used items easiest to access. Make a note in your planner two months from now to check this drawer for expired products.

Now, when you are doing your skin care and makeup, delight in the routine. When you are finished, become very present and aware of your breath. *This is the moment where you will create the new habit.* Instead of leaving the skin care items and makeup on the counter, you will now place them back in their new home: in the drawer. You slowly place each item in the drawer. Stop to smile at how they sit in there and close the drawer. Marvel with appreciation for how clear your countertop looks and take in how you feel now that your bathroom counters are not cluttered with items. Repeat the process tomorrow (conscious regular practice). Soon, your new habit will be formed, and the old ways will be gone forever. This process can be duplicated for any problem area of your home.

Notes

The Calm Key

"You cannot perceive beauty but with a serene mind."
—HENRY DAVID THOREAU

The motto of *The Daily Connoisseur* is "keep calm and remain classy." I like to say this at the end of my YouTube videos so we can all remember that calmness is key to success in life. This is certainly true for establishing method and order at home. The opposite of method and order is chaos, and chaos is the opposite of calm. Chaos is frenetic, disorderly, confusing, and unpredictable. When we forego our organizational systems, we are in a mild state of chaos. Instead of calmly placing the beauty items in the drawer, we leave them scattered on the counter. When establishing the new, positive habit, we must slow down, become aware of the present moment, and calmly execute the new action. This is how we will cement the newly established method and order in a positive way. This ultra-conscious state will make your new plan more successful.

COMMAND CENTER
MENU
MONDAY - Baked Cod
TUESDAY - Lettuce Wraps
WEDNESDAY - Turkey Bolognese
THURSDAY - Lentil Soup
RECIPE CARD
GROCERIES
Red Lentils
Olive Oil
MOM
DAD
JIMMY
EMMA
MON
TUES
WEDS
THURS
FRI
SAT
SUN
Birthday!
Pilates 5PM
PIANO After Sch
10AM DENTIST
Parkour
Lunch Ashley
FAMILY MOVIE NIGHT!
Church Picnic - Bring Blanket
BBQ
Keep Calm & Remain Classy!
TICKET ADMIT 1
Dear you are INVITED
2
Letters
BILLS
Mail

When we rush through our days unconsciously, we perform habits that rely on the previous rails we have laid down. Laying down new rails must be done consciously.

Here are a few tips on how to calmly integrate your new organizational methods:

Become aware of your breath. Breathe deeply and expansively when you are trying out the new habit. Breath awareness is one of the fastest ways to bring yourself into the present moment.

Be hyperaware of how you feel while performing the new habit. How does it feel to be where you are right now performing this different action? If it feels uncomfortable, ask yourself, why? Do you feel like this new method is a waste of time? Or does it feel uncomfortable because you've always done it a different way? Sink into those feelings of discomfort and don't ignore them. Facing these feelings are key to you expanding in this area and breaking through your limitations. If the new action feels good, notice that and revel in it.

Be aware of your tactile sensations. If you are putting your makeup away, for example, how do the cases feel to the touch? If you've ever seen an ASMR (Autonomous Sensory Meridian Response) video on YouTube, you'll notice a trend that many influencers will employ. Before using a product or putting it away, they will feel the product and/or tap it with their nails. This brings about a satisfying sound. I'm not suggesting you do this at home, but the idea here is to activate your senses, especially sound and touch, to make the process more memorable and positive.

Move slowly on purpose. By slowing down your movements, you counteract the state of rushing that might have characterized your earlier actions and habits. Sometimes, when presenting a tutorial online, the content creator might demonstrate the skill by showing it in slow motion. You can use this in your own life by moving slowly and purposefully. You don't need to do this forever, but you might find slowing down helpful at the beginning of your journey establishing the new habit.

Incorporate tranquility in your actions by feeling tranquil and soothed yourself. When used as a verb, the word calm means to make someone feel tranquil or to soothe them. You can do this by pushing all other nagging thoughts from your mind. If you are running late for work in the morning and feel tempted to leave all your beauty products out on the counter, invoke feelings of calm tranquility through breath, awareness, posture, and tactility, and assure yourself that putting the beauty items back in their proper place will only take a few seconds and that you have plenty of time.

If you feel a sense of urgency penetrating, businessman Matthew Weatherley-White suggests you bring your attention to steadying yourself and prioritizing calmness. That is the calm key, and it will aid you tremendously, not only with your life at home but in nearly every other area as well. Everyone likes to feel calm. Being calm feels safe, pleasant, soothing, and tranquil. When we feel calm while doing the new habit, we will naturally embrace it more because it feels good. Entering the present moment with a calm state of mind can only aid your new orderly habits.

A Connoisseur's Cleaning Routine

Ah, the cleaning routine. The necessity of every household. It doesn't matter if you do the cleaning entirely by yourself, have your family pitch in, or hire outside help; no matter what your situation is, you need a cleaning routine to run your home beautifully and efficiently. I have experienced all the scenarios of the routine over my adult life, everything from being solely responsible for the housekeeping to hiring professionals to help us. A regular routine that is rarely strayed from is the only way to go to keep everything running smoothly. Naturally, the routine can be malleable. There are some nonnegotiables (like keeping the kitchen and bathrooms clean for hygiene purposes), and other things can be let go during a crazy week. (It's okay if you didn't get to mopping the floor this week.) On weeks when you are feeling overwhelmed, the key is to prioritize what is truly important and what can wait. Think about the other routines in your life: your morning routine, for example. Likely, you have a set morning routine with activities you do every day, like brushing your teeth, washing your face, stretching, drinking coffee, and writing in a journal. On hectic mornings when unexpected events happen, you probably skip the stretching and journaling, but you would never skip brushing your teeth. No matter how your plans shift, that is a nonnegotiable for you. Our cleaning routine should have the same caveats. This helps when you are feeling overwhelmed with a difficult period of life.

SAMPLE CLEANING ROUTINE

Please note: Each day, the kitchen is cleaned after meals. This is a given and is not mentioned in the routine below.

Sunday: Rest
Monday: Wash towels and kitchen linens
Tuesday: Clean bathrooms, change bedding for half the house, vacuum
Wednesday: Mop floors, dust, do personal laundry
Thursday: Change bedding for the other half of the house, iron
Friday: Touch up bathrooms, wash towels and kitchen linens, vacuum
Saturday: Tackle bigger projects, mop floors

This is a sample cleaning routine, so please adjust it to meet your needs. You might have tasks to add to the list if you have lots of pets, or other special circumstances. Or if you live alone and only have one bed to change, for example, you can modify it to meet your requirements. The key to creating this bespoke routine is to peruse your schedule and make it fit your needs. Keep your commitments in mind when creating this routine. What is your work schedule? What is your school schedule? What about after-school activities? Do you wish to rest on the weekends with your family or do you prefer to get most of your cleaning done then so you can rest more during the week? This routine will be different for everyone. Journal about your ideal schedule and when these tasks can get done.

There is an old saying: energy flows where attention goes. When you put the energy into merging your cleaning routine with your schedule, powerful insights will come to you. You might become aware of a much better way to accomplish your chores. You might get ideas on how you can get more help or make the process more pleasant. Cleaning is not everyone's cup of tea. Most people despise it and would rather be doing something else, so it's only natural that you don't want to devote any more time to it than normal. But sift through those feelings and come up with a plan that will work for you.

Implement it and see how it goes. Make adjustments where necessary. Try to do this with a sense of joy and adventure.

Create your cleaning routine that meets your needs:

SUNDAY: ____________________

MONDAY: ____________________

TUESDAY: ____________________

WEDNESDAY: ____________________

THURSDAY: ____________________

FRIDAY: ____________________

SATURDAY: ____________________

TIME BLOCKING AND CLEANING

Time blocking is a planning technique that divides your day into blocks of time allocated to specific tasks. It is a wonderful technique for completing your to-do list and enjoying a well-rounded day. Time blocking works wonders for cleaning routines, too. If you're like me, once you start a task, you can get lost in it to the detriment of everything else you need to do in a day. To prevent this, time block your routine and set a timer. When the timer goes off, wrap up what you're doing and move on to the next task. This will aid you in completing all on your list.

For example, if you plan to do a general tidy of the downstairs living rooms including vacuuming, dusting, and organizing the toy room, plan to do it from 1:00 p.m. to 1:45 p.m. Once you know you only have 45 minutes to do it, you will aim to use the time efficiently and are less likely to procrastinate. When the timer goes off, you can calmly finish what you were doing and move on to the next thing. This allows you to see real progress. You won't get lost in the minutiae of the mission and forget to cook dinner or another important item on your to-do list and, thus, fall further behind.

Often, you'll find that you complete the task long before the timer goes off in your time block. This shows our propensity to overcalculate how long something will take us, which is probably why we dread doing it in the first place. If you find yourself with extra time, you have one of two options. You can carry on working until the timer goes off by going the extra mile. Get a head start on the laundry or do a task you've been meaning to do, like fertilize the houseplants. Or, you can add in some fun self-care time—read, sip a cup of tea, or watch a YouTube video—do something you've been wanting to do.

Time blocking can help you look forward to your cleaning routine. There's something comforting about knowing it won't take "forever" and that there is a light at the end of the tunnel. The task will end.

EMPLOYING PROFESSIONALS

For some people, employing professional housekeepers will be the answer to keep their home running efficiently. If you employ professionals, you still need to create a routine based on method and order so they can help you optimally. By sharing the needs of the home with your home cleaning professionals, together you can come up with an ideal schedule for them to implement. Unless your housekeepers come every day, you will still need to have a routine of your own to run the home on the days when they are not there. For example, if your housekeepers come twice a week on Tuesday and Friday to do most of the deep cleaning, you still need to keep the kitchen and bathrooms clean on days they are not there and likely also do the laundry. In this case, your cleaning routine will be modified but still stands. The bespoke cleaning method will be tailored to your exact needs no matter what your circumstance is.

SURVIVAL MODE CLEANING ROUTINES

Every household will go through phases of busyness and phases of calm. The child-rearing years are particularly challenging, and this is often when people will find themselves employing survival mode cleaning routines. The name is a bit deceptive because there is no "routine" in it to speak of. That's actually the problem. In survival mode, you just clean the thing that is the most urgent at the time and get by as best you can. Ultimately, the problem is there is *no* routine. But often, the person responsible for cleaning is too exhausted and overwhelmed to even think about implementing a routine. (Ask me how I know?) But the catch-22 is that the routine is what will set them free from this vicious cycle in the end. Once again, method and order come to the rescue. So, if you find yourself in survival mode cleaning, let's correct that. Make a cup of tea and use the previous section to come up with a Connoisseur Cleaning Routine that will give you freedom.

Before that happens, however, I need to share something. Every person goes through "rock bottom," otherwise known as "dark night of the soul," with their homemaking. During this phase, you might be dealing with sleeplessness, exhaustion, feelings of being overwhelmed, financial issues, health issues, relationship issues, parenting issues, or all the above! (That's what it felt like for me!) You *must* give yourself as much time as you need to work through those problems. Do not stress about keeping your home running in optimal order. Do whatever you can. So yes, survival mode cleaning is a valid and necessary tool for the darkest hours of our lives. I urge you to get the help you need to get through this period with support. Know that it will pass eventually, and you will have the energy to get excited about making your homelife as idyllic as possible again. This book will *always* be here for you when you are ready.

In my own rock bottom, I found myself exhausted with four children, homeschooling, working full-time, and running the home without help. My husband was shifting out of his current career while going through severe health problems. I would stay up until 11:00 p.m. working and get up at 5:00 a.m.

to continue work. At night, however, I wasn't sleeping well. I had interrupted sleep with a baby or toddler, and this went on for years. During the day, I crammed in homeschooling, housekeeping, and more work wherever I could. I was working myself to exhaustion. The entire time, I had such a strong desire to have a beautiful, well-run home. I did implement many systems, but I should have rested more or asked for help. I did not give myself the grace that I am asking you to give yourself. I pushed through when I should have rested and just allowed it all to crumble around me. Now, I can look back and see that. So, please do not feel pressure to start any of this if you are not ready or are going through a challenging time. Get the rest and help you need first. If you feel ready, however, and reading this excites you and lights a spark in your heart that you haven't felt in a while, that is your cue to begin.

The Joy of Doing

Cultivating a beautiful homelife is not always about lofty living. Yes, we take delight in our organized spaces, fashion together a gourmet meal with herbs from the garden, and arrange the roses in a charming bouquet, but we also need to mop the floor, clean out the refrigerator, and fold large piles of laundry. Is it possible to extract equal amounts of joy from our chores as we do from the pleasurable aspects of homelife? It is human nature to feel joyful and elevated vibrations from the tasks we deem enjoyable and to dread tasks we look upon as burdensome. But once we shift our thinking here and embrace all tasks at home as lovely adventures, we can truly settle into the joy of doing, no matter what.

The joy of doing is a phrase that has helped me cross this hurdle. It is deliciously ambiguous. The joy of doing . . . *what*? The "what" doesn't matter. It could also be called "the joy of doing anything" or "the joy of doing what you are currently doing." The French have a well-known expression "joie de vivre"

or *the joy of living*. The more precise translation: the exuberant enjoyment of life. *Exuberant*. What a great way to describe what we are going for. When you break down why you enjoy one task over another, it is truly about two things: feeling and thinking.

What is your favorite thing to do at home? How does it make you feel? I like going into the garden with my clippers and selecting flowers for a pretty bouquet. When I do this activity, I feel rested, creative, joyful, luxurious, and grateful. I feel rested because, when I'm in the garden, I naturally feel calm and as though I am "on a break." I feel creative because I get to work with color, texture, and scents to create a unique flower arrangement. I feel joyful because being around flowers makes me feel happy. I feel luxurious because I have a garden I get to tend, which seems like a luxury to me. And I feel grateful that I have this garden in the first place and can enjoy its fruits both outside and inside.

Taking this exercise a bit further, how do you feel when you are doing an activity at home that you don't enjoy as much? I'll give the example of laundry. Here is how I often feel when I am doing the laundry: overwhelmed, stressed, indignant, and as though I'd rather be doing something else. There is a definite "joy of doing" when I'm arranging flowers and a decided "dislike of doing" when I'm doing the laundry. The secret here is to transpose the feelings I get when I'm creating a bouquet from my garden by "cutting and pasting" them to my feelings about doing the laundry. This is where thinking comes in. Because of years of ingrained beliefs that creating bouquets is pleasurable and doing laundry isn't, my mind accepts the feelings associated with each task as fact. The way around this is to journal and meditate on these feelings and ultimately bring both acts into alignment with the joy of doing.

Journaling Prompt:

Write down your favorite activity to do at home. Then, write how you feel while you're doing it and why. Next, write down your least favorite task to do at home, how you feel when you're doing it, and why. Now, take that task and "cut and paste" the feelings from the first task to the second. Here is my journal entry with the examples I shared above:

> *I love picking flowers from my garden. I love arranging them into a bouquet that we can admire indoors. I feel rested, creative, joyful, and luxurious when I am clipping roses and creating my bouquets. I feel immense gratitude that I can enjoy fresh flowers daily and am constantly reminded of the magnificent beauty of nature.*
>
> *I dislike doing laundry. I feel overwhelmed while doing it because there are so many loads, and I never feel caught up. I am frequently stressed while doing laundry because I feel that I could be doing something more productive, pleasant, or exciting instead. I often feel indignant while folding large piles of laundry because I wonder why I am having to do this chore when I already do so much elsewhere.*

Solution: To ease the burden, find help with doing the laundry. If I cannot find help with it and must do it myself, I must change my feelings and mindset toward it. Is it possible to feel as happy about doing laundry as I feel about flower arranging?

I will now transpose my joyful feelings of flower arranging to my feelings of doing laundry:

I love doing laundry. I feel rested, creative, joyful, and luxurious when I am washing and folding our laundry. I feel grateful to have a washing machine and dryer to help make the process easier. I enjoy using the natural detergent that smells like lavender, which reminds me of our garden. I love feeling the softness of the sheets and towels as they come out of the dryer. I am appreciative that I can listen to my current audiobook while folding laundry, and the book makes the entire task more exciting. After doing laundry, I will get to rest by indulging in a cup of tea. I look forward to doing laundry again tomorrow.

Journal as long as you like on the subject and add as much flourish as you need to. It might feel as though you are "faking it until you make it" when speaking of your most dreaded tasks in this positive light, but you will be surprised at the new take on the task that truly takes over. You start to see all the enjoyable and positive aspects of the chore. Mentally, you can give yourself a shift and, over time, begin to believe the positive affirmation that you wrote. Another helpful idea is to read your positive journal entry right before engaging in the task as a reminder. You don't need to do this forever, but at least for the first week or two at the beginning of this experiment and any future date where you find yourself beginning to dread the task again. Soon, you'll find that you no longer hold that dread, and it is replaced with a true sense of gratitude and pleasure. You'll find the joy of doing laundry (or whatever your undesirable task is) much to your delight.

LET YOUR BODY SPEAK TO YOU

As you continue to infuse joy into all you do at home, make a habit of checking in with yourself and your body frequently. I find that my body is vocal when I'm doing something I don't enjoy. I will hold my breath, hunch my shoulders, tighten my stomach, and maybe even feel a little hot and flustered. These are cues to check in with myself. Why am I feeling this way? Do I need to take a break? Or do I need to pause and reevaluate how I'm regarding the task at hand? I recommend journaling about every task that you struggle with, not just your most dreaded tasks. Find as many positive things as possible about each task and expand on them in your writings. Let this be an ongoing process.

As you become better at listening to your body, you can take feelings of stress as instant opportunities to check in with yourself. You will begin to physically feel better over time as you become aware of these stress cues. If you notice you're holding your breath, make it a point to stop everything and take a few deep breaths to recalibrate. If you notice you are hunching your shoulders, do several arm circles forward and backward to open up your heart area and align yourself with proper posture. If you feel knots in your stomach, take a moment to breathe into those tight spaces and dispel the tension. After adjusting yourself physically, ask why your body experienced that tension. Make a note of it, and the next time you're engaging in that activity, consciously try to expand into it with free-flowing physicality.

THE DAILY ADVENTURE

In the book *Make Time* by Jake Knapp and John Zeratsky, the authors introduce The Daily Highlight as the most important task you will do in any given day. Doctor turned YouTuber Ali Abdaal calls it The Daily Adventure. While they are discussing the one major task of the day, you can also use this technique with all the microtasks you must tackle as well, especially the "undesirable" ones. So, cleaning out the refrigerator and restocking it with groceries can become an adventure as opposed to an activity you've been dreading. Find the joy of doing in everything that you do, and your homelife will improve dramatically.

EXUBERANT

Let's go back to that wonderful word: exuberant. The definition of exuberant is to be "filled with or characterized by a lively energy or excitement." It's truly the energy and feeling behind each activity we do each day that will qualify it as a joy or a dread in our minds. The joy of doing anything will cultivate the subtle energies of exuberance before, during, and after the task at hand. If you find yourself resisting what is and wishing you were doing something else, look into that. Now, the adventure begins. How can you alchemize these negative feelings into positive ones?

It is completely valid that you might be overwhelmed. It may be that you have too much on your to-do list or you are not getting enough help. So, feeling overwhelmed and negative about what you're doing should not be ignored. Before transposing your thoughts on each of your dreaded tasks, ask yourself if it is absolutely necessary that you do it. Could someone else do it for you? Either a hired employee or another member of the household? If that answer is yes, then off-load it from your to-do list by delegating the task. But if you and only you must do the chore, then it is your duty to make the best of it and reframe it to become pleasant. This small but mighty change will improve your entire day. ◈

The Joy of Being

We must not get so wrapped up in the busyness of everyday homelife that we forget to pause and relish the present. To explain, here the flipside to the joy of doing can be found in the joy of being. There likely will never be a day when you don't have something on your to-do list at home. There will always be home-related activities to keep us busy. The key to my happiness at home is not constantly losing myself in these activities. Cultivating the joy of doing whatever task I'm engaged in is a key to being happy in the present moment, but sometimes, a deeper exploration is needed so that my life isn't one never-ending to-do list. The joy of being at home is an art unto itself. When I think about the chief aim of my home-related tasks, the higher idea is that I am doing them so my homelife will ultimately be delightful. Occasionally stepping off that path to enjoy my homelife as it exists will allow the pleasure to sink in deeper. It is appreciating the endgame without needing to be at the end.

The joy of being can be found in accepting what is. That might be a home with a finished to-do list, with gleaming counters and freshly made bread. Or it could also be luxuriating in the cozy fire even though there are toys strewn about the floor and a sink full of dirty dishes. In these moments, allow the distraction of the unfinished task list to fade into the background as you focus in on the crackling flames of the fire. Feel the warmth on your skin as you fully immerse yourself in the pleasure of the hearth. Rather than seeing your houseplants and worrying that their leaves need dusting, stop to admire their beauty: the poetic way the leaves have turned toward the window seeking light. Instead of noticing all the sticky handprints on your French doors, focus on the beauty of their architecture as the threshold between home and garden. Never forget to take these moments and appreciate the higher aspect of home and each element in its grandest form.

The joy of being is about presence, breath, and appreciation.

The more you can appreciate your space as it currently is, not wishing for it to be different or "finished," the more joy you can find in being where you are. And when being turns to doing, you can enter the activity with great peace and purpose.

Journaling Prompt:

Step into a room of your choosing and write down why you love being there. How do you feel in this room? What is the higher idea of the space? How can you call in gratitude to appreciate it as it is? What do you enjoy about simply being in your home? How can you carry this joy with you all throughout the day?

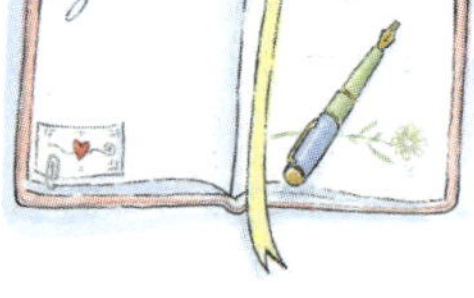

MAKING IT FUN

After implementing your routine, how can you stick to it? The only way, I have found, is to make it as pleasant as possible so you actually look forward to your housekeeping. The following tips all require a change in perspective. If you view your cleaning tasks as inevitable drudgery and allow dread to penetrate your being when faced with them, you will have a miserable time. But if cleaning becomes an opportunity to better yourself and your home, your negative outlook flips, and suddenly, the tasks become more enjoyable.

The single most effective way to make housekeeping more gratifying is to give yourself audible treats while cleaning. Listen to your favorite podcast, a riveting audiobook, motivational music, or chat on the phone with your best friend while you're doing it. Any of these can make folding a giant pile of laundry or tackling a daunting living room disaster zone more satisfying. I have found that when I am listening to a good audiobook, I'll go above and beyond in my cleaning just because I don't want to pause the book! If I'm listening to an educational podcast, I feel like I am investing in self-improvement while also being productive with the housework. If I listen to motivational music and happen to dance while cleaning, I'm getting a workout in (more on this to come). If I'm catching up with a good friend on the phone, I feel like I'm not alone while cleaning.

When you employ any of these auditory treats, your time-blocked chores will not only go by quickly, but you will look forward to this time where you can simultaneously beautify your home and better yourself.

As mentioned, another way to enjoy cleaning more is to see it as added exercise in your life. In *Lessons from Madame Chic*, I share the insights I learned while living in Paris. One major lesson was that exercise was a part of life, not a chore. The French people I observed did not go to a gym, but rather incorporated exercise into their daily life through walking, using the stairs, and yes, housekeeping. The French are not alone in this. In Dan Buettner's groundbreaking research on the "blue zones," where people live the longest on the planet, he reveals that many of the people experiencing longevity actively participate in the cleaning of their own house. In the article "Make Your Home a Calorie-Burning Haven" on Buettner's website bluezones.com, it says, "*By spending just two hours working in your yard and two hours cleaning your home each week, you'll burn approximately 1,150 extra calories per week. Keep that up all year, and you'll lose 17 pounds—without dieting or going to the gym.*"

That statistic alone is enough to motivate many people who wish to get more physical exercise but don't have time to go to the gym. If you look at housekeeping as a creative way to get in exercise, you might look forward to it more. So, instead of "having to" bend down to pick up cereal off the floor, you can do your squats to get there. Instead of walking around the kitchen to put the dishes away, you can dance while you do it—just don't drop your dishes! Instead of lugging the vacuum around the living room, you can push it out with intention as you would a rowing machine at the gym. Engage your core while you do this and feel gratitude that you are agile enough to do these movements and clean your home.

Another technique is to welcome the before and after reveal. Most people love watching a good old-fashioned transformation, whether it's a makeover or a redecorating project. When you are cleaning, take in the "before," not with a feeling of dread but by dwelling in the possibility of what it can become. Emily Dickinson wrote, "*I dwell in Possibility, a fairer House than Prose.*" Sure, your kitchen might look like a code-red disaster, but don't let that get you down. Envision yourself relishing a cup of tea with your favorite magazine in a clean kitchen. Then, roll up your sleeves, don your rubber gloves, and make the possibility a reality. When the kitchen is clean, don't forget to allow a moment to take it all in. This is the "after" reveal, and those are always so deeply satisfying.

A final way to enjoy housekeeping is to reward yourself. This is the "dangling carrot" at the end of the stick, and there's no shame in following it. I like to plan these rewards and schedule them in my planner. After cleaning the bathroom, for example, watch a video from your favorite YouTuber (ahem), or that show you can't get enough of on Netflix. Or partake in a cup of tea and a slice of cake. Lay out in the garden or take a nap! The treat must speak to you as something you can get excited about. Set goals for yourself and regular breaks and treats to incentivize your tasks which will make the whole experience more pleasant.

Notes

Notes

Dining Well

Arguably, one of the most important tenants of fine living is dining well for each meal. When we visit hotels and restaurants while traveling, we expect the best from our food. How much more important is it to dine well at home where most of our meals are consumed? Dining well is not something that happens by accident but is the product of planning and implementation. In other words, *Method* and *Order* to the rescue!

Growing up, my mother always had a delicious meal ready for us every evening. I wanted to provide the same thing for my family. After running a household of six people and needing to provide regular healthy meals over many years, I have learned much about how to go about doing it and certainly have a greater appreciation for what my mom did for us. Cooking a fresh meal from scratch like my mom did is definitely ideal. But for modern-day busy life, such luxury is not always available. The following are my best tips for preparing your meals ahead of time so that even on your busiest days, when you don't have time to cook a fresh meal, you will still dine well at home.

MEAL PLANNING

The most important aspect to get right is the meal plan. You can be as detailed as you like, but I find that creating a plan and holding it loosely is what works for our family. Let's say you are responsible for providing seven healthy dinners in a week, and you are going to cook four of them (I'll explain where the other three are coming from later). Take some time to write down and plan what those four meals will be. You could write them in a meal planning notebook, on the kitchen command center menu, or anywhere that suits you. Once you know what you're making, check to see what ingredients you already have in your kitchen and what you'll need to purchase fresh from the store. Plan this all before your meal prep day. By planning ahead (method) you set yourself up for success. Then, you can go to the grocery store or have your groceries delivered and get ready to implement your plan (order).

MEAL PREPPING

Having a regular meal prep day where you get a lot of the hard cooking work out of the way in one afternoon is a magnificent strategy for keeping consistent with serving healthy meals. You've planned your menu and ordered your groceries, and you are ready to go. On meal prep day, you will not only prep all four meals but likely will share one of the meals that very day. When I'm in the kitchen cooking, I like to get as much done as possible. My philosophy is: if I'm getting the kitchen messy, I might as well go all out! Oddly enough, this keeps the kitchen tidier throughout the week. If you are constantly bringing out the pots and pans to cook things here and there, there is more cleanup to do at the end of the cooking session, but when you've already done all the cooking on one day and you are merely reheating, you don't make as much of a mess.

Here is a sample menu with four dinners for the week and how I would implement them through meal prep:

Baked Cod in Foil Packets

Makes 4 servings

This is one of the easiest ways to prepare fish, and there are infinite variations on what you can do. The cleanup is very easy, too!

Extra-virgin olive oil
2 cups prepared vegetables, divided
4 cod fillets
1 lemon, sliced
1 handful chopped herbs
Salt and ground black pepper, to taste

Preheat the oven to 400°F. Create four foil packets by placing four equal squares of aluminum foil on two baking trays. Drizzle or spray the foil packets with olive oil. Place ½ cup prepared vegetables in the center of each foil packet. Place sturdier vegetables, like zucchini, bell pepper, carrot, and green beans, on bottom and save more delicate vegetables, like cherry tomatoes, on top of the fish. Place 1 fillet of cod (or your desired fish) in each packet. Season with salt and black pepper. Top with lemon slices, herbs, and a further drizzle of olive oil. Seal the foil packet. Roast the fish packets on baking trays in the oven for 20 minutes or until the fish is fully cooked. Eat alone or serve over hot rice.

Prep for Ground Turkey: ***The next two recipes use ground turkey. If preparing on meal prep day, take 2 large onions (chopped), 6 cloves garlic (minced), 2 pounds ground turkey, and ¾ cup diced carrots. Cook the onions and garlic in olive oil over medium heat until softened. Add the ground turkey and cook until brown and fully cooked through. Add diced carrots and continue to cook for 5 minutes. Season with a dash of garlic salt. Drain. Divide the turkey in half: one portion for the lettuce wraps and one portion for the Bolognese sauce. You can fully make each sauce on meal prep day to save extra time on the days you eat the meals, or just prepare the meat in advance to make it all go smoothly on the day of. It's up to you!***

Ground Turkey Lettuce Wraps

Makes 6 to 8 wraps

This is a crowd-pleasing dish for both adults and children. It's fun to eat with your hands, and everyone can make their own!

1 tablespoon extra-virgin olive oil
1 pound cooked ground turkey, onion, garlic, and carrot mixture (from meal prep day)
⅓ cup hoisin sauce
1 tablespoon rice wine vinegar
3 tablespoons soy sauce
2 teaspoons sesame oil
1 (6-ounce) can chopped water chestnuts, drained
4 green onions, chopped
1 head butter lettuce

Place oil in a saucepan over medium heat and reheat the ground turkey, onion, garlic, and carrot mixture you prepared on meal prep day. Add hoisin sauce, rice wine vinegar, soy sauce, sesame oil, water chestnuts, and green onions. Stir until sauce is fully combined and meat is thoroughly reheated. Serve in butter lettuce leaves.

Easy Turkey Bolognese

Makes 6 servings

A traditional Bolognese is made lighter with the use of turkey here. This is a family favorite and one that my kids never tire of eating.

2 tablespoons extra-virgin olive oil
1 pound cooked ground turkey, onion, garlic, and carrot mixture (from meal prep day)
2 cups water
1 (28-ounce) can whole tomatoes
2 (16-ounce) cans tomato sauce
2 tablespoons tomato paste
2 teaspoons dried basil
2 teaspoons dried oregano
2 teaspoons garlic salt
Ground black pepper, to taste
1 pound cooked spaghetti
Parmesan cheese, to garnish

Heat oil in a large saucepan over medium heat, and add the cooked ground turkey, onion, garlic, and carrot mixture from meal prep day. Add the 2 cups water, whole tomatoes, tomato sauce, tomato paste, herbs, garlic salt, and pepper and cook on medium-low for about 20 minutes. Serve over hot cooked spaghetti and garnish with grated Parmesan cheese, if desired.

Notes____

Red Lentils

Makes 4 to 6 servings

Having a meatless item on your meal prep list always makes life easier. This is my favorite red lentil dish, and I make it several times a month.

1 small onion, chopped
3 cloves garlic, minced
2 stalks celery, chopped
2 carrots, chopped
1 tablespoon extra-virgin olive oil
2 cups red lentils
6 cups vegetable or chicken broth
1 handful chopped fresh herbs
Salt and ground black pepper, to taste

Over medium heat, sauté onion, garlic, celery, and carrot in olive oil until softened. Add 2 cups rinsed red lentils. Add 6 cups broth along with some chopped herbs. Cook on low for 15 to 20 minutes. Season with salt and pepper and serve over rice.

Notes

MEAL PREP NOTES

On meal prep day, I tend to serve the menu item that doesn't keep the longest, which is the fish dish in the menu on the previous pages, so we would have the cod. In addition to getting everything out for that meal, I also begin to cook the ground turkey in batches for both the lettuce wraps and Bolognese. Once the ground turkey is cooked, I divide the meat for the two meals and season accordingly. The idea is to make as much in advance on this day as possible (sealable containers are the key to keeping the prepped food fresh). Meal prepping is a fine art that requires finesse, flexibility, and bespoke touches. Take into consideration how much time and energy you have and do as much as you can to make your week of fine dining go smoothly.

OUTSOURCE TO AVOID FEELING OVERWHELMED

A meal plan is a great idea but what happens if you burn out from cooking so much? Even a meal plan can't help you there. Sometimes, you just need a break. I typically do not cook every meal each week. I did that for a long time. Actually, I cooked three meals a day every day for our large family for many years, and it was too much for me. I know many a home cook that relishes this challenge, but I listened to my body, and after going through a period of intense burnout, I realized that the responsibility of cooking every meal without a break was a tremendous burden, and I needed to off-load some of the work.

I have used meal delivery services where ready-made meals are delivered to our home; I have had family members be responsible for cooking a meal, and I have also employed the help of household staff to help with the meal prep. Since off-loading a portion of the cooking each week, I have been able to take a "breather," and when it's my turn to step up to the plate and cook the meal, I am in there, with an enthusiasm that would make Julia Child proud, making delicious meals and enjoying every minute of it. My experience and feeling of cooking burnout might not be your experience. But it is important to honor your true feelings, if you are overwhelmed, and find a way to give yourself a break.

Other ways I have lessened the load of cooking three meals a day involve empowering your family members to create their own meals. Breakfast is a wonderful meal to implement with this. Teach your children how to create a healthy breakfast on their own. My daughters have been making their own breakfasts for years. And they don't just pour a bowl of stale cereal. They make healthy smoothies, eggs, yogurt parfaits, and avocado toast. They love having the breakfast they crave, and I don't feel overwhelmed like a short-order cook, making several different breakfasts. Encouraging your children to make their own meals isn't neglecting them but rather empowers them to learn how to take care of themselves and dine well from a young age.

FREEZER MEALS

Another meal planning strategy to consider is freezer meals. So many meals freeze well and can be brought out on busy days when you do not have time to cook a homemade meal. If you are making a cottage pie, for example, why not make three: one for tonight and two for the freezer? You can tailor your meal prep days to accommodate freezer meals. When I make freezer meals, I feel so accomplished and ahead. Some of the best meals/foods that freeze well are also family favorites:

- *Chicken Pot Pie*
- *Green Chicken Enchilada Casserole*
- *Slow Cooker Chicken Chili*
- *Cottage Pie*
- *Beef Tips*
- *Taco Soup*
- *Beef Bolognese Sauce*
- *Coconut Chicken Curry*

Chicken Pot Pie

Makes 3 freezer meals

½ cup (1 stick) salted butter
1 large onion, chopped
½ cup all-purpose flour
2 cups chicken broth
2 cups milk
6 cups veggies (I use steamed carrots, celery, cooked potato, and frozen sweet corn, but use any combination you like.)
4 to 6 cups shredded cooked chicken
Salt and ground black pepper, to taste
6 piecrusts (prepackaged or homemade)

Melt butter in a large pot and add the chopped onion. Stir until the onion is soft. To create a béchamel sauce, add the flour and cook until the flour is dissolved. Now, add 2 cups chicken broth and 2 cups milk. Stir until creamy, about 5 minutes. Add your veggies to the creamy béchamel sauce and stir. Then, add the shredded chicken, salt, and pepper.

Tip: To easily make shredded chicken, place 4 to 6 chicken breasts in the slow cooker with about 2 cups chicken broth and cook on low overnight, for 8 hours. When you wake up, you can shred the chicken with a fork. Reserve the broth for cooking the pot pie later.

Distribute the filling into 3 pie tins each lined with 1 piecrust. Place 1 piecrust on the top of each, trim the edges with a knife, and seal with a fork around the perimeter of the crust. Cut some slits into the top to vent.

Chicken Pot Pie continued . . .

To prepare the pies for the freezer, cover them in plastic wrap and aluminum foil. If you use plastic wrap, don't forget that it's there. Be sure to remove it before popping it into the oven!

To cook a pie, let it thaw in the refrigerator overnight. The next day, bake the pie at 350°F for 1 hour. Leave a layer of foil on the pie for the first 30 minutes so the crust doesn't burn.

To cook the pie from frozen, bake at 350°F for 1 hour and 30 minutes. All ovens are different, so you will need to check the pie and add time as needed.

You may brush an egg white or some melted butter on the top crust to make it golden brown.

Alternative method: Instead of preparing the entire pie for the freezer, I have also frozen the filling separately in freezer bags. When it comes time to bake, simply thaw the filling overnight in the fridge and then place in a piecrust and bake as usual the day you would like to have the meal. There are many variations on making this that will make your cooking experience efficient. This chicken pot pie is so delicious! Served with a salad, it makes a hearty meal.

Notes

Green Chicken Enchilada Casserole

Makes 2 casseroles

1 tablespoon extra-virgin olive oil
1 large onion, chopped
6 cups shredded cooked chicken
2 (28-ounce) cans green enchilada sauce
6 cups chopped fresh greens (spinach, kale, or Swiss chard)
1 handful fresh cilantro, chopped
Salt and ground black pepper, to taste
10 to 12 corn tortillas
3 cups shredded Monterey Jack cheese
Green salsa, sour cream, sliced green onions, cilantro, to garnish

Heat the olive oil in a large pot and cook the chopped onion until tender, about 5 minutes. Add 6 cups shredded chicken and stir to incorporate. Add 2 cans green enchilada sauce. Stir. Add 6 cups chopped greens, cilantro, salt, and pepper. Cook over medium heat until the greens have cooked down. Now, assemble the casseroles. Start with a layer of the chicken mixture as a base, then add a layer of corn tortillas. Add a layer of the chicken mixture and then sprinkle the cheese on top of that. Repeat until you reach the top of the casserole, finishing with a sprinkle of cheese on top.

To prepare for the freezer, cover the baking dish with aluminum foil.

To cook, thaw in the refrigerator overnight. Bake at 350°F for 1 hour.

To cook from frozen, bake at 350°F for 1 hour and 30 minutes, making sure to check that the casserole is cooked through before serving.

This is delicious served with green salsa and sour cream. Garnish with chopped cilantro and chopped green onion.

Slow Cooker Chicken Chili

Makes 2 freezer meals

3 to 4 cups shredded cooked chicken
2 (15-ounce) cans tomato sauce
1 large onion, chopped
1 tablespoon minced garlic
1 (15-ounce) can white cannellini beans
1 (15-ounce) can red kidney beans
2 to 3 cups chopped greens (spinach or kale)

Place all ingredients in a gallon-size freezer bag. When ready to cook, thaw in the refrigerator overnight. Place in the slow cooker in the morning. Cook on low for 8 hours, or high for 4 hours. Serve with sour cream, shredded Cheddar cheese, and chopped green onion. Please note: you could easily make this with ground beef instead of chicken.

Notes

Cottage Pie

Makes 3 large pies or 6 small pies

1 large onion, chopped
2 tablespoons extra-virgin olive oil
6 pounds ground beef
4 (6-ounce) cans tomato paste
3 tablespoons bouillon (chicken, beef, or vegetable)
3 tablespoons all-purpose flour
3 cups broth
1 cup water
Salt and ground black pepper, to taste
4 to 6 cups frozen mixed vegetables
6 cups mashed potatoes
Shredded Parmesan cheese, to sprinkle

Cook the chopped onion with a few tablespoons of olive oil on medium-high heat in a large pot until the onion is soft, about 5 minutes. Place the ground beef into pot and cook until brown. Drain the fat from the cooked meat and return the meat to the pan. Add the tomato paste and stir. Add the bouillon and flour and stir until incorporated. Add 3 cups broth and 1 cup water. Season with salt and pepper, if desired. Cook for 5 to 10 minutes more, but do not allow the mixture to get too dry.

Divide the meat mixture in the bottom of 3 baking pans (or 6 small pans for smaller portions). On top of that, place a layer of frozen mixed vegetables (or you could use frozen corn, or any combination of chopped fresh vegetables). Finally, spread a layer of mashed potatoes on top. I like to make my mashed potatoes the day before so there is not too much work to do the day of assembly.

Cottage Pie continued . . .

To freeze: Cover your pans with aluminum foil and label them with the date and cooking instructions.

To cook: Thaw in the refrigerator the night before. Then bake at 350°F for 1 hour, or until the pie is fully heated through.

To cook from frozen: Place frozen pie in the oven and bake at 350°F for 1 hour and 30 minutes. Add additional time, if needed, to cook thoroughly.

You may sprinkle Parmesan cheese on top if you wish. It's nice to place the pie under the broiler for 1 minute before serving to make it golden brown.

Notes

Beef Tips

Makes 3 freezer meals

3 pounds beef stew meat
2 cups beef broth
2 cans cream of mushroom soup
1 large onion, chopped
2 cups chopped button mushrooms
2 tablespoons chopped garlic
½ cup brown gravy mix

Mix together all ingredients in a large mixing bowl. Divide equally among 3 freezer bags. Label and freeze.

To cook: Thaw overnight in the refrigerator. Place in a slow cooker on low for 8 hours or in an electric pressure cooker (like Instant Pot) on high pressure for 30 minutes. Serve with chopped parsley over rice, mashed potatoes, or hot buttered noodles.

Notes

Taco Soup

Makes 3 freezer meals

2 tablespoons extra-virgin olive oil
1 large onion, chopped
2 stalks celery, chopped
5 pounds ground turkey
¾ cup taco seasoning
1 (16-ounce) can chili beans with liquid
2 (15-ounce) cans tomato sauce (or diced tomatoes)
2 (16-ounce) cans kidney beans, drained
2 cups frozen corn
2 cups water
2 (4-ounce) cans diced green chili peppers
½ cup salsa verde
4 cups fresh greens (spinach, Swiss chard, or kale)
1 bell pepper, chopped
Salt and ground black pepper, to taste
Garnish: shredded cheese, sour cream, avocado, tortilla strips

In a large stockpot, heat the oil on medium heat. Cook the onion and celery until soft, about 5 minutes. Add the ground turkey and cook until brown. Drain. Add the rest of the ingredients and let simmer for at least 30 to 40 minutes. Let the entire soup cool. Divide the soup into gallon-size freezer bags. This should make about 3 to 4 freezer meals. Label and freeze.

To cook: Thaw in the refrigerator overnight. Place in the slow cooker on low for 8 hours or in an electric pressure cooker (like Instant Pot) on high pressure for 30 minutes. Serve with shredded cheese, sour cream, sliced avocado, and tortilla strips.

Beef Bolognese Sauce

Makes 2 freezer meals

1 tablespoon extra-virgin olive oil
1 large onion, chopped
4 cloves garlic, crushed
2 pounds ground beef
2 teaspoons Morton Season-All (or salt and ground black pepper to taste)
2 (28-ounce) cans whole tomatoes
2 (15-ounce) cans tomato sauce
2 tablespoons Italian herb seasoning

Cook the onion in oil in a large pot over medium heat for 5 minutes or until softened. Add the garlic and cook for 1 minute more. Add ground beef and cook until brown. Drain the fat and return the meat to the pan. Add Season-All, canned tomatoes, and tomato sauce to the pan, stir until combined. Stir in Italian herb seasoning and simmer on low for 30 minutes. Add water if the sauce cooks down too much. Allow to cool. Divide the sauce between 2 gallon-sized freezer bags. Label and freeze.

To cook: Thaw in the refrigerator overnight. Place in a slow cooker and cook on high for 3 hours or low for 8 hours. Cook spaghetti according to the package instructions. Once cooked, drain and add to sauce. Serve with shredded Parmesan cheese and a side of garlic bread.

Even if you have not planned an organized meal prep day, always consider doubling the batch for whatever meal you're making if it freezes well. This way, you can at least serve one meal and save one for later.

Coconut Chicken Curry

Makes 4 to 6 servings

1 large onion, chopped
2 to 3 carrots, chopped
2 to 3 potatoes, peeled and chopped into large chunks
1 handful fresh cilantro, chopped
1 pound chicken breast, chopped into bite-sized pieces
1 red bell pepper, chopped
1 (14-ounce) can coconut milk
1½ cups chicken broth
1 tablespoon curry powder
Salt and ground black pepper, to taste

If you are making this for the freezer, combine all ingredients in gallon-size freezer bag. Label, date, and place in the freezer. When you are ready to cook the curry, thaw in the refrigerator overnight. Place in a slow cooker on low heat for 8 hours or on high heat for 3 to 4 hours. When the curry is finished, serve over hot rice with extra chopped cilantro on top. Feel free to substitute vegetables as needed.

Notes ________________________________

EMPOWER AND RELINQUISH

Once you have established the method and order needed to create regular, healthful meals, you have laid the foundation for family fine dining. You will get in a rhythm that will free up more time to take this new element of home living to the next level. You may even feel inspired to dress the table with linens, tablecloths, and nice dishes to elevate the dining experience. Fresh flowers from the garden will grace your table, and the clutter in the surrounding area will be cleared to further enhance the atmosphere of your dining area. Call upon the feelings evoked when dining at your favorite hotel or restaurant and recreate them at home. We will explore this in greater detail in later sections of the book.

Notes

Homemaking Failures

I have had my fair share of homemaking failures in my adult life, and when I look back on them, there seems to be one common denominator present: I was rushing. Before I unpack that revelation, let me tell you about some of my recent failures.

It all started with the potatoes. Interested in cultivating my own potatoes, I set out on a journey to grow my own heirloom varieties. I had a few successes with the potatoes in my kitchen garden, but there was a lack of space, so I thought I'd try the clever hack of growing the potatoes in grow bags. I purchased the bags on the Internet. They were dark green and even had a little "peek pouch" below so I could check on the potatoes' progress. This was very appealing to me as my problem was not knowing quite when the potatoes were ready. I did everything the instructions said and nurtured them for two months, checking them diligently and making sure I was doing everything right. Checking the pouch a few times after the prerequisite 60 days, I decided my beautiful heirloom potatoes were ready for harvesting. I picked them ceremoniously and thought up dishes I could use them in. Sure, they seemed a bit puny, but I had grown these spuds, and I was proud of my first effort. I brought them into the kitchen and scrubbed all the dirt off them and placed them to dry in a kitchen rag that I set off to the side. Then, I got distracted. I can't remember with what, but I'm sure I started helping my children do something. Then, one thing led to another. The afternoon was full, as it always is. My children were younger then, so I was very involved with helping them with day-to-day things. I cleaned the house a bit, put in a load of laundry, and began cooking dinner, the usual culprits. I was trying to get all the chores done so I could rest a bit before bed. At the end of the day, I felt exhausted, but I remembered I needed to put the laundry into the dryer. I opened the washing machine and was perplexed to see a little brown lump mixed among the kitchen linens. And then, with disbelief, I dug a bit more only to find *all* the heirloom potatoes I harvested had gone through the wash cycle! How did they end up there?! Looking back, I realized, when I was gathering the kitchen linens for the

wash, I must have swiped the cloth holding the potatoes into the basket, forgetting my little pride and joys were in there. This triggered a laughing fit and near nervous breakdown in me. I had taken so much time over the past two months to protect and nurture my potatoes. I had so many plans for them! I was going to make French *pommes de terre* with butter and herbs. I had been filming the process for YouTube, so not only were my family and I looking forward to these potatoes but thousands of other people across the world were, too. And here they were all soapy and bloated from one hour in the wash cycle. Sigh.

While I am on a roll, let me tell you some more homemaking "fails" so we can further see the common thread. One day last summer, I was in a rush (I know . . . what a shock!) trying to do everything I needed to do before leaving the house. It was bed-linens day, so I took my sheets off the bed and put them in the washing machine on the bedding cycle. Then, I went about the rest of my morning, managing my family's needs and responding to work emails that needed to be dealt with from my laptop. Time went by, and I started gathering everything I needed to leave the house. But where was my iPhone? I couldn't find it anywhere. I couldn't ask my husband to call it because he was out of town. I searched all the usual spots, and it was nowhere to be found. A feeling of mild horror overtook me. Did

I accidentally put my phone in the washing machine? No, that would be impossible. I think I would notice my heavy iPhone amidst my bedding, wouldn't I? But all the same, I opened the washer and stared. The hot, soapy water was all the way to the top as I had interrupted the cycle. I reached my arm down and tried feeling around for my phone, but the heavy duvet cover and sheets didn't reveal anything. I closed the lid, continued the wash cycle, and resumed my search. Frustrated that I could not find my iPhone, when the wash cycle was finished, I went back to check. I pulled out all the wet bedding to put it in the dryer and (yes, you guessed correctly) my iPhone was sitting at the bottom of the basin, sea-weary and thoroughly waterlogged. It had been through one hour of hot water, detergent-infused soaking, and tumbling.

And now, here's my third story, which also had to do with the laundry (my Achilles heel). About a year later, I was washing my bedding again on a busy morning. When the wash cycle was finished, I transferred my sheets to the dryer and turned it on. Before leaving for the morning, I stopped the dryer halfway through to fluff the sheets. I don't like when they get into a tangled ball and dry unevenly. But when I opened the dryer, I noticed black spots all over my white bedding. At first, I thought it was lint, but upon closer inspection, I realized the sheets were stained. Perplexed, I pulled my bedding out onto the floor of the laundry room. The more I inspected, the worse the stains became. Giant black blobs were splattered in large spots all over my high-quality bedding. Even my silk pillowcase was covered in spots! I pulled out the culprit: a black pen I had journaled with that morning. I sometimes journal in bed as part of my morning routine, and, while I usually put my pen back on my nightstand, I had forgotten this time.

My final homemaking fail doesn't have to do with the laundry (what a relief!). I was preparing lunch quickly because I had a Zoom call scheduled with my channel membership group on YouTube, The Chic Society. Our calls last for one hour, so I wanted to have lunch beforehand. I boiled a pound of pasta and made a quick sauce. With an eye on the time, as soon as the pasta was finished cooking, I poured it into the colander in the sink to drain the water. When I went to transfer the drained pasta to the casserole dish, I was in such a rush that I comically missed the dish, and the entire pound of pasta I had just boiled went straight into the sink, mostly down the drain. I did that thing one does in disbelief where I wondered for a brief moment if I could salvage it, but I knew I couldn't. Wow. One pound of pasta wasted. I had barely enough time to make more, so I did and scarfed down my lunch before the call, but my stomach didn't like the rapid eating.

These homemaking fails have brought a few things to my attention:

1. Shake and thoroughly inspect your laundry before putting it in the wash. (You'd think I would have learned this after the potato incident but apparently not!)

2. Try to put things back right away and not save that task for later. With the potatoes, I should have dried them thoroughly and put them on the cutting board or in a bowl. My phone and pen should have gone on my dresser after use.

3. Be calm in your movements. After draining the pasta, I was almost there. A calm and controlled action of pouring the pasta into the casserole dish would have required slowing down a few seconds.

4. Don't rush! Why am I rushing? I feel like I need to pack so much into every moment of the day for ultimate productivity. Rushing is not only counterproductive but also expensive! The iPhone and ink fails were pricey. I had to replace my

phone (thankfully, I had insurance but still had to pay some fees), and the ink incident required me to buy all new bedding. The potatoes were "expensive" in that it cost time to nurture them. And wasting one pound of fresh pasta is terribly annoying as I hate wasting food. All this rushing did not promote productivity but set me back significantly.

5. The final and most important lesson I learned from these failures was that, when they happen, there are only two things you can do: laugh and learn! Mistakes are going to happen. Especially when you are running a home. Eventually, rushing or multiple responsibilities will cause you to slip up. So, being perfect and never making mistakes are not the goal. The goal is to pause when these mishaps occur and learn from them. Why did they happen? What is the greater lesson to grasp from them? My lessons involve not rushing through my day and not valuing productivity over all else. The motto of my channel is "keep calm and remain classy," and I needed to heed that in my homemaking, too. So, not only learning from the incident but being able to laugh about it is key for me as well. The mad laughter that poured from me after the potato caper was so therapeutic. While I didn't feel like laughing immediately after the iPhone, pen, and pasta incidents, I was able to look back and laugh. I don't need to take myself so seriously. These homemaking escapades held a lot of wisdom and have caused me to grow.

Journaling Prompt:

What have been your biggest homemaking fails? Write them all down. Is there a common thread? Did they all involve a certain activity (like the laundry or cooking)? Were you rushing through all of them or not paying attention, not being present in the moment? Why did they occur? Can you laugh about it now? What can you learn from these incidents?

Final Thoughts on Method & Order

I have shared many scenarios in this book that I have encountered on my homemaking journey, but no two experiences will be alike. I encourage you to dig deeply into your own daily life and solve all the mysteries behind why your homelife isn't ideal. Getting honest and working on these areas will be rewarding. I like to think of it like playing a difficult piece of music on the piano. When I come across a few bars of music that are challenging to me, I slow down and go over and over them until I play the part correctly. Then, I play the piece correctly over and over again until the correct way to play it has been ingrained. The next time I sit down at the piano to play, I get to the challenging part, and it is no longer a problem. What a feeling of satisfaction and accomplishment! Working out our own home dilemmas can be equally fulfilling. Tackle the "difficult section" of your homemaking and go over and over it again until the proper bespoke method and order have been established. Then, continue to concentrate on it until your new habit rails are laid down and the problem no longer exists. The method and order are there to serve as the foundation for beautiful living. Please remember to enjoy this process as it can be highly pleasurable. Now that we have established method and order to run our home joyously and efficiently, let's focus on adding all the beautiful details into our daily living. Are you ready? This is going to be even more fun!

Notes

Notes

PART II:
BEAUTY

 Decorating the Home 

"I am going to make everything around me beautiful—that will be my life."

—ELSIE DE WOLFE

Fine living is not only about having a beautiful home, as many would think, but it also encompasses how we exist in our homes: how we present ourselves, the activities we do there, and the special touches that make everyday life extraordinary. This section will cover all the ways you can take your now highly functioning home up a few notches by focusing on beautiful living in all its glorious aspects.

I need not expend too much energy convincing you that decorating your home is a fun process. This is something almost everyone gets excited about. The good news is that the foundational elements of running your home have now been implemented so you can enjoy your beautifully decorated home even more. But let's not get ahead of ourselves. First, let's assess your situation. Is your home decorated to your tastes? If so, you can read this section with nostalgia or amusement. If your home is not decorated to your tastes, ask yourself why? What is holding you back from decorating the way you want to? Is your budget holding you back? Are you worried that bold decorating choices will affect the resale value of your home? Are you a renter, and you're not sure how much you're allowed to decorate? Do you feel intimidated by interior design and are not sure what your style even is? Answering these questions will reveal a lot of limiting beliefs you have surrounding your home décor.

My husband and I held off on decorating our first home for many years because we were worried about resale value. I wanted to add wallpaper and other custom touches that I didn't think other people would like but I bought into the idea that the more neutral we kept our home, the easier it would be to sell when we wanted to do so. The trouble is that we lived in this first home for several years without decorating and only upgraded a few things (like the kitchen and bathrooms) right before we did eventually sell. So, the entire time we lived there, we were not enjoying our home aesthetically because we were scared. Realizing the years wasted, I recognized the absurdity of this mindset, and when we moved into our second home,

I wallpapered, added bold curtains, and made other touches to the garden without fear of resell value. Ironically, we didn't stay in the home very long and found ourselves selling it only two years after we bought it. Even more ironically, the lady who bought our home told our agent that the reasons why she bought it (in addition to being in the right location for her) was that she loved the wallpaper and curtains I had put up! So, there went my theory that bold design choices would hinder resale value.

When we moved into our third home, I knew I was not going to mess around with waiting any longer to express our true style. No matter what the future held, no matter how long we planned to stay there, we were going to decorate according to our tastes and live every day inspired and pleased by what we saw. We began by redoing our kitchen and installing wallpaper in key rooms like the bedrooms and dining room. There were a few rooms that we held off on decorating simply because we were stumped by what to do in those spaces. But that was the only reason, not because we were afraid the home wouldn't sell again one day. After careful thought and consideration, when we finally knew what we wanted to do in those rooms, we implemented the designs and were (and continue to be) so happy with how it turned out. It's important to mention that this was all done on a tight budget, too.

From Builder-Grade to Jewel Box

"Bloom where you are planted."

—SAINT FRANCIS DE SALES

Let me tell you more about the home we live in now—the one we decided to decorate to our tastes. Several years ago, my husband and I made a decision that many families make. We decided to leave the city (Los Angeles) and move to the suburbs. City life was lovely for us as a married couple, but once we had children, there were many aspects of living we longed for that we did not have access to in the city. We wanted a private garden, a swimming pool, and a safe neighborhood where our kids could play outside with other children their age. We wanted a place where there was less traffic and abundant (free) parking, and where the cost of living was more affordable. We moved back to the town where I grew up, which is about a one-hour outside of Los Angeles. It's funny how life brings you full circle. After I graduated from high school, I could not wait to hightail out of my small town and head for the city, and now, I was longing to go back and live a slower-paced life in the cozy and familiar town of my youth.

Moving to the suburbs was one of the best decisions we made. I instantly felt deep relief at experiencing all the changes we had been longing for. I loved and appreciated our new home. It was right near my parents, and we lived on a safe street full of friendly neighbors and children who our kids loved to play with. But, of course, not everything was perfect. We lived in a typical suburban tract where the houses were all "builder-grade," and every fourth house looked the same. Some would call them "cookie-cutter houses." I appreciate individuality in design and have a deep love for older homes

(I dream of living in a Victorian house one day), so moving into such a generic and bland home presented some challenges. We made certain changes right away, and as our budget allowed, we slowly decorated room by room, turning our generic builder-grade home into a beautiful jewel box that charms and delights us every day. Even if you do not live in a builder-grade home, I hope the next section inspires you to decorate to your tastes without reservation.

WHAT IS A JEWEL BOX?

We all know what a builder-grade house is: cheap, boring, generic, common, standard, and uninspired. But what is a jewel box home? Though typically descriptive of a smaller home, jewel box design can be applied to any home you live in, whether a tiny apartment or a large mansion. Think of the nicest jewelry box you've ever seen. Chances are it was beautifully designed in all aspects, from the exterior of the box to the interior. I have a few jewelry boxes that double as music boxes. They have beautiful veneers on the outside, and when you open them, everything commands your admiration, from the engraving on the inside lid to the quilted cushion on the bottom of the box. I wanted a jewel box home where every room you walked into was beautifully designed from the floor to ceiling, a home reminiscent of an exquisitely decorated dollhouse.

Keeping this goal in mind, our formerly builder-grade home has been transformed into a jewel box through wallpaper, moldings, curtains, colorful cabinetry, custom murals, and more. Walking inside feels like a trip to a beautiful, cozy, and whimsical fairy-tale home. You would never know it was builder-grade. What are our secrets? Here are the main ways we transformed our space from builder-grade to jewel box and the lessons I learned along the way.

PLANT EARLY

The first area I upgraded was the garden. Plants are relatively inexpensive, and when we first moved in, we were on a tight budget, so adding to the garden was a way to feel like I was making design strides without spending too much money. This proved to be a wise decision because plants take years to mature, and getting started right away is the best way to guarantee beauty sooner. The previous owners had planted several rosebushes in the front yard as well as crepe myrtle trees in the back that erupted into glorious pink blooms that gave us privacy from the houses above. But other than that, the garden was not very special as there was an abundance of concrete with not a lot of greenery. Knowing that time was of the essence, I took to planting several of my favorite plants in the back garden with the hope that, in a few years' time, they would take off profusely. I planted bougainvillea, French lavender, pink and yellow lantana, star jasmine, lemon and fig trees. In addition, we planted plum, peach, and bay leaf trees and put in privacy hedges on either side of our fence to wall us in with a "secret garden" feel. It took a few years, but the plants took off in abundance, and now each spring, when you walk onto our patio, the previously barren space is awash with a literal wall of blooms, with hot pink bougainvillea reaching in cascades over bushes of lavender. It feels like you're in the South of France, not a suburb in Southern California. The bees, butterflies, birds, and dragonflies are certainly happy, too. The takeaway? Begin planting right away and then be patient. Plants take time to mature, but when they do, the luxury you feel from your bountiful garden is unparalleled.

UPGRADE WHAT YOU ALREADY HAVE

Our kitchen had a typical '90s design with brown cabinets and brown granite. The room felt dark and dated. The appliances were starting to fail, too, so we decided to upgrade the kitchen as our first interior project. Being on a budget, however, we did not have the luxury of ripping out the cabinets to install custom ones, so we worked with what we had. We kept the builder-grade cabinets that came with the kitchen but had the doors to the cabinets replaced and painted in a fresh duck egg blue with new copper handles installed. The brown granite countertop was replaced with white quartz, and we got all new appliances. Keeping the old cabinets saved us thousands of dollars, allowed us to use our budget to upgrade the appliances and countertop, and fulfilled the pleasing aesthetic I was seeking in a new kitchen.

One of the best transformations for the kitchen came in the dining section. Previously, it housed a bar area with seating right next to the kitchen table area. Tall barstools loomed over the lower kitchen table, crowding the space. It all felt so cluttered. We eliminated the dueling seating areas by turning the barstool area into a custom bench with storage. The bench acted as seating for one side of the large kitchen table, and another bench was placed on the other side. Now, the kitchen table was the only star of the show, and we could all sit down together comfortably without the barstools crowding us out. This is a prime example of "solving a problem" by making it beautiful and functional. Now, we love to sit around the kitchen table, and there's plenty of room without two seating spaces in competition with each other. Upgrading what we already had in the kitchen proved to be a design choice that worked within our budget to wonderful results. As I write this, it's been several years since we upgraded the design, and not a day goes by that I don't walk into my kitchen and love it.

WALLPAPER

One of the best ways to customize your home and make it unique is through wallpaper. Builder-grade rooms are usually blank boxes with no special architectural details or interest. After our kitchen renovation, we had four rooms wallpapered: the primary bedroom, our daughters' rooms, and the dining room. We chose a traditional blue-and-white toile de Jouy depicting a French country scene from the 1700s for the primary bedroom. The wallpaper instantly transformed the otherwise boxy space into a beautiful French retreat. The girls' rooms have sweet florals that brightened up the drab walls, and the dining room, draped in Cole & Son Winter Birds wallpaper, makes you feel as though you are dining in an enchanted forest.

The interior of a jewel box is usually an ornate space with every area enclosed with beauty. The use of a wallcovering brings out this special jewel box feel by enclosing you in an enchanting pattern or scene. When selecting wallpaper, choose prints that speak to your interests in soothing colors you love. Think of the room you're papering to also inform your choices. Dining rooms might call for more bold and dramatic wallpaper, whereas bedrooms might require more delicate, peaceful patterns.

If you're worried that a wallcovering will affect the resale value of your home, remember that our second home sold partially because the buyer loved our wallpaper. Worst-case

scenario would be that you take it down and paint the walls white if you feel like it's necessary in order to sell. But you might not need to. Renters can take heart in the plethora of peel-and-stick wallpapers on the market that can easily be removed. It is always advisable to ask your landlord's permission before installing, but wallpaper can now be for everyone, enhancing our rooms and upgrading them to jewel box status.

ADD ARCHITECTURAL DETAILS IN

Builder-grade houses usually do not have any special architectural details to speak of. You're lucky if you get an arched doorway or a column here and there. So, architectural accents must be added. One easy way is to add wainscoting panels that are attached to the lower part of a wall in a room. Wainscoting presents a wonderful opportunity to add interest to your home. One of the most popular methods of creating wainscoting is to keep the lower paneling white while painting or wallpapering the upper part of the wall in a different color or pattern. But there are truly no rules. You can paint or wallpaper the wainscoting on the bottom, if desired, and do a contrasting color or paper on top. Our bland upstairs hallway was a labyrinth of beige walls. We had wainscoting panels installed on the lower part of the walls, had them painted white (Benjamin Moore's Swiss Coffee to be exact), and then had Evergreen Fog by

Sherwin-Williams, a moody green, painted on the top half of the walls. Our hallways went from boring to elegant when we made this transition. The wainscoting added architectural interest that elevated the space.

Focus on the positive aspects of the architecture in your home and find a way to enhance it. Our front drawing room has a very high ceiling that stretches up to the second floor. I loved the high ceilings, but we were perplexed on how to decorate them. Our walls were painted beige, the color that came with the home when we bought it, so we had beige walls that went up two stories high with a few paintings hung up to human height. I was stumped for years by what to do in this space. All I knew is that I wanted a change. After watching countless YouTube videos on interior design and pouring through books, I decided upon wall paneling. Wall paneling could add definition and interest to the walls and make the high ceilings feel grand and special. Because the walls were so long, we could also get away with a richer color than beige. We eventually had the walls painted in the same Evergreen Fog we had used upstairs. Along with the wall paneling, the new green walls provided the single most dramatic design shift in the house. Now, when people walk in, they are met with the grandeur of the high ceilings (the design element I always loved), but the color and paneling brought out this wonderful element and made the room special. Adding architectural detail through wall paneling instantly upgraded the rooms from builder-grade to jewel box. You feel as though the paneling has been there all along!

MURALS

Feeling emboldened by the results of our other decorating projects, I continued in my desire to transform our generic rooms into spectacular spaces. Our powder room was the most boring, builder-grade room you could imagine. Builder-grade fixtures, a neutral mossy beige color on the walls, and flickering strip lighting. I have always appreciated powder rooms with charm and whimsy and lamented the lack of design in ours. Ripping out the bathroom and replacing it with a new one was not in our budget, so I turned to creativity and art to give it a jewel box feel. I love chinoiserie and have always admired wallpapers and art in this genre. I knew a very talented artist and commissioned her to create a custom chinoiserie mural in our bathroom. Our contractor painted the walls in Sherwin-Williams' Aristocrat Peach, and our muralist went to work to create the most enchanting forest scene with flowering trees, birds, and butterflies. Our contractor painted our travertine tiles in a cream and matcha-green harlequin pattern (which required sanding and an epoxy coating) and painted the trim and door in the same matcha-green color. The change to this small space is dramatic, whimsical, custom, and oh-so-surprising to everyone who walks in. It has transformed from a generic space lacking inspiration into an enchanting and expensive-looking powder room. The most ironic thing about it is that our builder-grade bathroom is now one of a kind; it's the only one in the world like it, thanks to our custom mural.

We loved the bathroom mural so much we commissioned the artist to create another chinoiserie mural on a grander scale in our family room. Inspired by chinoiserie and the enchanted forest theme, she created a mural with beautiful trees, plants, flowers, rolling hills, and wildlife (a peacock, crane, butterflies, and hummingbird among some of the stars). When you walk into our living room, you are at once transported to this peaceful and exotic garden. We added curtains, upgraded some of the furniture, and layered rugs for softness. This previously generic space is now magazine-worthy. The older I get, the bolder and more unapologetic my interior design choices have become. Limiting myself with neutral decorations for so long has unleashed my inner flair for ornate interiors.

THE FUN IS IN THE CHALLENGE

I gained many valuable insights from the ongoing transformation of our home. Instead of wallowing in regret that our home didn't come with more beautiful architectural details, I learned to revel in the process of creating a customized domain. It is unrealistic to think that everyone in the world will get to move into a home beautifully decorated, exactly to their taste. In fact, that is probably a scenario that rarely happens. The wonderful challenge is looking at your space, envisioning how you want it to be, and coming up with creative ideas on how to change it within your budget. One could argue that a builder-grade space is easier to upgrade as it acts as a "blank canvas." Using wall paneling, wallpaper, and paint to transform what you have not only creates a beautiful space in which you can thrive but also is a tremendously rewarding process.

A WORD ON BUDGETS

For many people, the budget will be the most hindering factor to decorating, but I urge you to think creatively here. Write down everything you'd like to do to your home. For many options, you can recreate your favorite looks on a budget, by either doing them yourself or finding contractors willing to work with the budget you have. Where there's a will, there's a way! With our murals, for example, we found a local artist who was able to work within our budget. If you're longing for a mural, seek out local artisans or consider that someone in your own family may be a talented artist. See what you can do to make it happen.

Journaling Prompt:

What is your vision for your home? How can you redecorate your space to meet your vision? How can you do this in a way that fits in your budget?

SPACE	BUDGET

The View

Picture this: You get dressed up to go to your favorite restaurant. This establishment has beautiful ocean views and delicious food. You can't wait. You arrive at the restaurant, and the hostess asks you to follow her as she walks you to your table. She leads you past the tables near the expansive window with the ocean view and keeps walking toward the back of the restaurant. She seats you at the farthest table in the room, against a dark wall. The revolving door to the bathroom is right next to you. Are you happy with this table? No! You want to sit at one of those lovely tables you walked past earlier against the large window that has an unobstructed view of the ocean.

Or what about this scenario: You book a hotel room at the seaside. This is your long, awaited vacation. You've been looking forward to this occasion all year. The bellhop escorts you to your room. As soon as you step out of the elevator, he turns to the first door to the left of the lift. You have a slightly panicked feeling. Why did they give you the room next to the elevator? Are the noises from this high-traffic area going to keep you up at night? You decide to give it the benefit of the doubt and see the room. You walk in, and he pulls open the curtains to reveal a prime view of the parking lot. All you see is oil-stained concrete and cars. This is not what you signed up for. You want the ocean view from your balcony, far away from the dinging of the elevator. It's time to make a call to the front desk.

Why does the view matter? Because whether you are dining at a restaurant or booking a hotel room, you want the experience to be the best possible one. You're not only in it for the good food and comfortable bed, but you also want the entire package. You want your eyes to be pleased as well. We should keep these high standards when we are in our homes, too, and optimize the view whenever we can.

OPTIMIZE YOUR VIEW

Ideally, every window in our home will have a pleasant view, but the views that are the most important and take priority are the spaces where we linger the most: views from the tables we dine at and views from our bedroom, which are the first we see every day. This is quite a fun challenge. Look out your window. What do you see? Brainstorm or journal about how you can optimize this view. If you see a plain concrete patio, perhaps you can bring beautiful potted plants so you can have a "garden" view. Or if your window looks out onto a wall, perhaps you can grow a climbing vine up the wall to add some greenery.

The view from our dining room is the front yard. We previously had beautiful crepe myrtle trees that bloomed a few times a year as our view, but a windstorm came through town and blew down our trees. We now had an unobstructed view of our neighbors' front yards, which left us little privacy and made our home feel very exposed. Our solution? We drove to the garden center and bought a few mature trees of mid-height that now block the view to their homes. Our pretty view is restored.

The view from the primary bedroom is my favorite in the house. It overlooks the pool and the expansive slope that is planted with flowering trees, bougainvillea, irises, and lavender. During the spring, the flowers overwhelm the space in the most spectacular way. It is the first view I see when I wake up. During the fall months, the flowering trees bloom, continuing the cascades of blossoms. Even in the winter, when many of the plants are barren, I appreciate the scale of these large trees and the view of the dormant pool.

Quick Fix Tip: Sometimes, what will fix your view is not entirely in the budget. For example, our poolside furniture had gotten a bit shabby, but

> new patio furniture would cost thousands of dollars. We were using our budget in different ways to upgrade other areas of the house, and updating the patio furniture was not a priority for us. I found some inexpensive blue-and-white striped towel covers to hide the drab lounge chairs. The inexpensive upgrade gave the space a much-needed lift and matched our blue-and-white striped umbrellas. Now, when we look out onto the pool, we see these cabana stripes and feel like we are at a posh resort!

In another window to our side kitchen garden, we had a view of a wooden fence. My husband installed arches in the raised beds, and I planted grape vines and climbing roses on them. So now, our view is of these enchanting plants. Creating a beautiful view is a wonderful challenge. ❖

Journaling Prompt:

How can you improve your views at home? What would you do if you could do anything and cost wasn't a factor? How can you achieve this and keep on budget? What are the most memorable views you've seen in your life? What feeling does a good view give you? Do you expect to have this feeling at home?

Dressing Well at Home

We have been placing much thought into making our homes presentable through cleaning, decorating, and organizing; now, let's turn that creative eye around. How do you present yourself at home? Think of yourself as an ornament in your home. You are also a part of the atmosphere, and much more important than any books, knickknacks, or pieces of furniture. Your essence and energy are what permeate the space in a meaningful way. Yet, it is a common choice for people to dress well when leaving the house but not when residing at home. Many people dress in old clothing that has seen better days because they feel comfortable in these pieces. The older, worn clothing is soft from much use, and they might feel like they can relax more in them. Or the clothing allows them to harken back to former glory days (old concert T-shirts or clothing from college or the adolescent period). But this dual mindset, of wanting to be presentable in public but not at home, is detrimental to living well. You are living a mixed message that your homelife should be excellent but does not require the respect of dressing well for it. I used to deal with this very mindset and know from experience that the only way to amend it is to identify the limiting beliefs you hold about your self-worth and shift those beliefs to align with your true desires.

The first limiting belief to banish is that appearing presentable means being uncomfortable. The desire to change out of tighter, constricting clothing once home, in favor of soft, cozy clothing, is perfectly acceptable. The new, expanded idea to adopt is that presentable clothing can also be comfortable. Modern loungewear comes in many different varieties and is as comfortable as pajamas or your favorite workout clothing. You can find pants, skirts, dresses, shorts, kaftans, tees, blouses, sweaters, and any manner of clothing with elastic waists and soft linings to make you feel exceptionally comfortable. These items are highly flattering and presentable, too. They can also be found at any price point. The key here is to wear loungewear that is intentional. Often, the sloppy clothing worn at home is put together without thought of how it looks or wears. But cream jogger pants paired with a soft cream sweater, for example, or a brightly colored kaftan and house slippers can express your style elegantly without sacrificing comfort. Set aside a budget to find presentable loungewear that you can get excited about wearing around the house. If you have a more formal style and enjoy wearing your day clothing at home (instead of wearing loungewear), you have even more options to dress your best at home.

The second limiting belief to dismiss is that dressing well takes too much effort. This idea is easily debunked because it takes the same amount of energy to put on one outfit as it does to put on another. Getting dressed in a presentable way is no less taxing than wearing your old favorites. The expanded idea here is that dressing well is not only easy but gives you added energy and enthusiasm for your day. You might experience resistance at first when choosing to express your style at home, but you will also notice a distinct energy boost from dressing well. Even when you are alone, you will feel a marked difference. There is something thrilling about presenting well for yourself and no one else. You are telling yourself that you are worth the conscious effort and that your style is worthy of being expressed. If you wake up and put on a breezy summer dress, for example, you might feel energized to handle all your activities for the day ahead. But if you stay in your pajamas, which are not presentable and make you feel tired and frumpy, you will find that you feel low and unmotivated. To make this shift easier, come up with an easy-to-implement dressing and grooming

routine. Always keep your presentable clothing accessible and give away your unpresentable items, thereby not even allowing yourself the temptation of wearing them. Over time, you will notice a distinct shift in your attitudes on dress. You will feel an energized joy from dressing in your style and begin to feel uncomfortable if you slip back into wearing your unsightly clothes out of habit. Once this shift has occurred, you will likely not go back to the old ways. You have leveled up your personal appearance to match the vibration of your home.

The third limiting belief to dispel is that you are not seeing anyone at home, so what's the point of getting dressed? The expanded belief here is that you alone are worth dressing well because it is a sign of your dignity and a creative expression. This does not mean that your clothes must be expensive or on-trend; it simply means that you consciously wear clothing that expresses your style in a way that is aesthetically pleasing to you because it is your right to express yourself. How we live at home, behind closed doors when no one is looking, is our true self. When you are not putting on airs for other people or pretending to be someone you're not just to impress, you are at your most comfortable and authentic self. When you decide, as this self, to dress well for no other reason than to express and live your authenticity, you are aligning with your beautiful desires. The added benefit of dressing well for yourself is that you will be prepared for any situations that arise throughout the day. If you do have an unexpected visitor, you can welcome them in with confidence without worrying about your appearance. If you have an impromptu video call for work, you can take it without reservation and not scramble to put yourself together. If you don't see or interact with anyone the entire day, you can move through your day knowing with dignity that your efforts are good enough for you alone.

Journaling Prompt:

If you feel resistance to dressing well at home, ask yourself why? Do you own comfortable clothing that is also presentable? What does feeling comfortable mean to you? How can you align being comfortable with expressing your style consciously? If you were to design your ideal outfit to wear at home, what would it look like? Who are some of your style icons? Can you find images of them on social media that show how they dress at home? What inspiration can you take from these images? When you dress well at home, how does it affect your day?

___

___

___ *(keep writing on next page!)*

Dressing Well Tip: Don't tempt yourself to wear clothing that isn't suitable. Anything you own that is too worn or shouldn't be worn by you, get rid of it. Don't even give yourself the option of wearing it. Many people will keep these items, saying they can do the gardening in them or any messy DIY projects. Set aside some of your presentable options for those occasions and get rid of anything you'd be embarrassed being seen in public wearing.

PRESENTABLE SLEEPWEAR

The same principle holds for your sleepwear. Wearing presentable sleepwear is another crucial component of living well at home. When you choose to dress well, you are suggesting that homelife is worthy of dressing well. Sloppy dressing will no longer feel good to you. Your home is running so beautifully and decorated so stylishly that you will also want to elevate your own appearance. This is not to suggest that you should become self-conscious or high-maintenance in any way. But as you uplevel your life at home, your sleeping attire will also feel like it needs an upgrade. Presentable pajamas are a wonderful gateway to boosting self-esteem. Yes, you are sleeping most of the time you are in them, but by wearing comfortable sleepwear that expresses your tastes, you are putting together the final puzzle piece of beautiful self-presentation.

I underwent this awakening when I was living in Paris, and I realized that my sloppy sleepwear was not in alignment with the elegant lady I wished to be. Once I began to wear presentable pajamas, I never looked back, and no matter how tired I am at the end of the day, I feel great slipping into something pretty and elegant.

You can find presentable pajamas at all different price points. Here are various styles to consider:

The Long Set: Pajama pants and a top that are coordinated to go together are great for colder nights. The top can be long-sleeved, short-sleeved, or sleeveless.

The Short Set: A pair of shorts and a top in a coordinating color or pattern are great for warmer nights.

The Chemise: Usually short, light, and breezy, the chemise is pretty, romantic, and perfect for hot nights or feeling cool under a heavy duvet.

The Nightgown: The more elegant counterpart to the chemise, nightgowns are usually midi or floor-length. They can have long or short sleeves or be sleeveless.

The Dressing Gown: A dressing gown is an elegant cover-up for your pajamas. Dressing gowns can be light in fabric or made of thick velvet, for example. Chic kimonos make excellent dressing gowns and cover any type of pajamas beautifully.

The Bathrobe: Bathrobes are usually made of thicker fabric and are often lined with absorbent material to keep you dry after the bath. They are great for colder months when you would like to be warmer around the house.

Slippers: A comfortable shoe that is worn indoors, slippers are not only functional with non-slip soles, but also charming and whimsical. In the warmer months, consider open-toed slippers to keep your feet cool and fleece-lined slippers to keep your toes warm in the fall and winter.

Journaling Prompt:

How does it feel when you wear pajamas that align with your style? Do you have resistance to wearing your pretty sleepwear? Do you feel like you need to save them for a special occasion like holidays or when visiting family? What would happen if you wore your favorite sleepwear on a nightly basis? How does wearing presentable sleepwear affect the rest of your day? If you were to design your ideal pair of pajamas, what would they look like?

AN INTENTIONAL WARDROBE

Becoming intentional about how you dress will be easier to achieve each day.

Here are my top tips:

Only display the current season you're in. Place all out-of-season clothing in storage bags or a guest closet. By doing this, you will cut down on the choice fatigue that comes from selecting your outfits every day by homing in on only the available options.

Discard or donate all items that are unsightly or no longer reflect your true style. This will prevent temptation for slipping back into undesirable dressing patterns.

Arrange your clothing as if you were curating a chic boutique. This will get you excited about the clothes you already have by creating a similar visual impact to walking into your favorite shop. You can arrange clothes by color, style, or item.

Matching velvet, wood, or padded hangers are a must to keep your clothes in good shape and provide a uniform look.

Use canvas bins to store out-of-season clothing, extras, or items that are not hangable. Label each bin according to what's inside: swim, exercise, sweaters, scarves, etc.

Keep pajamas seasonal to encourage wearing your nice ones daily. Keep one or two dressing gowns or kimonos to cover up when you are chilly.

Keep your clothes hamper nearby to avoid laundry spilling over onto the floor. Create a system each week to do your laundry, press, and put it away. Make it an enjoyable process by making it a ritual you can look forward to.

Keep a handheld steamer near your wardrobe so you can easily steam items when you are unable to iron.

A lint roller and sweater fabric shaver are invaluable items for keeping clothes in top shape and should be kept near the steamer.

To learn more about the wardrobe, check out my YouTube channel, *The Daily Connoisseur*, read my Madame Chic books, or watch my TEDx talk.

Notes

Notes

Dining Well— The Details

In Part I of this book, we discussed the method and order behind dining well. Once you get organized and routinely make healthful meals through planning, prepping, freezing, and outsourcing, you will experience delicious food in no time. Another aspect to consider with fine dining is all the other elements that make mealtime special. What is the atmosphere like during your repast? If you have prepared a delicious roast chicken dinner with seasonable vegetables and a glass of wine, will you enjoy it if you're sitting at a table full of clutter while the TV is blaring the nightly news? Not likely. If your dining circumstances are less than ideal, you have the wonderful opportunity to change them. I get an absolute joy from setting a beautiful table for each meal. The view, lighting, and sound are all key elements, too. Think of your favorite restaurant. What are the elements this restaurant employs to make the dining experience pleasurable? Likely, the seating is comfortable; the lighting is just right, and the music adds to the mood of the evening. What can you do to make your dining area feel this luxurious when you're having your meals?

> **"There is nothing like staying at home for real comfort."**
>
> —JANE AUSTEN

TABLE LINENS

The easiest place to begin is with the table itself. Clear all clutter from the dining table. You should never be competing with non-dining related items when you're enjoying your meals. Use tablecloths, place mats, or chargers to dress the table. Cloth napkins make a fine addition as well. Find dishes and glassware that express your style and go with your home's feel. As a dishware enthusiast, I love to change our dishes out each season, but you can use simple white plates and still create an elegant look. A centerpiece of simple flowers from the garden or anything that touches your fancy also goes a long way to making the table elegant.

Here are a few ideas for centerpieces:

A simple bouquet of flowers
A bowl of lemons or limes
Small potted plants
Hurricane candleholders with candles
Pillar candles

Table Linens Tip: Set the table the night before for breakfast the next day. Choose the linens and make sure the table is ready for a new day of meals. Savor the creative process of making the table attractive. When you wake up, you'll feel as if your personal butler has done this for you!

LIGHTING

Dining under blazing harsh lighting is a rather unpleasant experience. While you don't need to dine by candlelight every evening (although you certainly could), options to soften the lighting go a long way. Our dining room chandelier is on a dimmer switch so we can lower the lights as the night goes on. Tapered candles are always an elegant touch, especially in the winter months.

SOUND

A peaceful dining atmosphere is so important. I love listening to classical music while eating. This instantly elevates the atmosphere and makes me feel peaceful and relaxed. Of course, there will be the odd evening when cartoons are playing in the background because it's just been "one of those days," but in general, we should be very present while eating and not engrossed in watching TV, especially watching anything upsetting like the nightly news or an intense thriller.

YOUR STATE OF BEING

While you are eating, it's important to be in a calm, peaceful state. This is why we should not be watching the news or anything upsetting while we are ingesting food. Not only that, but we should avoid upsetting or stressful discussions. I noticed a terrible habit I had and recently amended it. Because the whole family gathered at dinnertime and we were all in one place, I found myself constantly going over the upcoming schedule with the kids and reminding them about what they needed to do. One day, I realized how unpleasant it must be for the kids to be thinking about their schedules while they are trying to eat. I caught my bad habit and decided to not do that anymore. Now, we just engage in pleasant conversation and tell each other about our day and whatever we like to share that is on our minds. It's a good idea to watch yourself and notice what you tend to bring up at dinner. If you're stressing your family out like I was, put all scheduling aside and simply enjoy your dinner, allowing you and your family to nourish yourselves in a peaceful environment.

> **Dining Well Tip:** Get in the habit of walking after dinner. Take in the sights of your neighborhood, burn off calories, and get some fresh air. Walking after dinner can help aid digestion and assist with

maintaining a healthy weight. It's also a great way to explore your neighborhood and be familiar with your neighbors and surroundings. A nice chat with a neighbor after dinner helps build a sense of community.

Notes

Exercising Well

Many will go through phases of time when it is not possible to get to a gym or an exercise class. Busy work schedules, lack of childcare, or even tight budgets can contribute to missing out. Luckily, exercising at home is easier than it has ever been. There are so many resources for at-home workouts. Find the right ones for you. I do a combination of rebounder, at-home workouts, swimming, and walking. It's a well-rounded routine that I look forward to. If you are someone who likes to frequent a gym but find yourself needing to work out at home, reflect on your favorite aspects of gym life and try to incorporate them into your own home. Consider creating a gym for yourself in the garage, an unused guest bedroom, or an outdoor space that works. Equip yourself with the exercise equipment that you need, put up a mirror, and set yourself up for success at home. I personally love a good view when working out, so I situate my rebounder to allow me to see the garden as I jump. If I am outside on a mild day, I place it in the garden with a view of the pool. If I am doing an at-home workout, I usually like to also listen to an audiobook to keep me entertained. Create an ideal atmosphere that will make you want to exercise at home and not only love it but look forward to it, too.

Create your workout regimen that fits your schedule:

SUNDAY:
MONDAY:
TUESDAY:
WEDNESDAY:
THURSDAY:
FRIDAY:
SATURDAY:

High-Quality Leisure

**"If you are losing your leisure, look out!
It may be that you are losing your soul."**
—VIRGINIA WOOLF

The beautiful life at home includes high-quality leisure. With the modern temptation to binge-watch television shows and scroll endlessly on social media, one must fight to secure high-quality downtime. If you have found yourself in this situation, enjoy the process of reclaiming enriching hobbies. For as you do so, you claim back your power as well. Quality leisure pursuits at home will be different for every person, but the one key aspect it will have in common is that it will be a highly conscious choice (as opposed to mindless scrolling or binge-watching) that will enrich your life. It will feel expansive and right. If your days are categorized by busyness, work high-quality leisure into your schedule slowly and incrementally. Write it down on your to-do list and schedule it in your planner. Make time for it and stick to the method and order behind introducing it into your life again. Adulthood might have taken this from you. You might be busy working a full-time job, raising children, tending to your home, and all manner of things. Your level of exhaustion might feel so overwhelming that all you can picture yourself doing is collapsing on the sofa in front of a show. Those days are called for. But check in with your heart and tell yourself the truth about what you truly miss. What brought you joy as a child or young adult? What would happen if you made time for that again? When you begin to reclaim your quality leisure time, you might raise some eyebrows from friends and family. This is because you are transforming before their eyes, becoming who you fully want to be, and they are noticing. Here are some high-quality leisure activities to do at home. As you read, notice if any of these activities get you excited or bring about a sense of nostalgia. I encourage you to write down your own favored activities if you do not find them here.

READING

Arguably the highest of high-quality leisure activities, reading should feature on everyone's priority list. When I was in my self-proclaimed busiest phase of life, I told myself I didn't have time to read books; I could only listen to audiobooks while I did activities around the house. But I missed the truly luxurious feeling of curling up with a good book with reading as the primary (not secondary) action. Treat yourself to the joy of reading again. Read in the garden, read in your armchair, read in the bath, or read in bed. Reading expands your mind and puts life in perspective. There is always time for reading.

GAMES

Chess, backgammon, card games, board games, crossword puzzles, and jigsaw puzzles, whether played solo, with a partner, or in a whole group of people, are wonderful for leisure time as they foster connection, laughter, concentration, joy, and healthy competitiveness. High-quality leisure activities will often develop desirable attributes in your character, and many of these games improve creativity, problem-solving, and concentration. If you are feeling burnt-out from staring at screens too much each day, games are a wonderful escape.

PLAYING AN INSTRUMENT

Whether it's the piano, guitar, harp, ukulele, or the flute you played in high school, experience the thrill from picking up a beloved instrument again and challenging yourself to play it. Or if you are playing for the first time, value the process of learning. Consider lessons to keep yourself accountable with an in-person lesson or remote online course. Schedule the same time every day to work on your craft. The meditative quality of playing music reduces stress and promotes patience and perseverance.

ART

Whether watercolor, oil painting, drawing, sketching, sculpting or any other artistic medium: engage in artwork that enriches your soul. If creating art is a part of the way you express yourself, it is imperative that you make time for it in your life. I have never fancied myself an artistic person in this sense, but a friend challenged me to do a watercolor. It was liberating to spend an afternoon creating a watercolor scene. I felt a sense of accomplishment in creating something beautiful. This experience prompted me to begin drawing tutorials with my children, and we often enjoy spending our evenings filling our sketchbooks with new creations. Create art for yourself and don't worry about public opinion. Get lost in the joy of creating and knowing you are the only person on earth qualified to make this piece. Keep a sketchbook handy for drawings.

JOURNALING

There are many types of journals you can keep: daily diaries, gratitude journals, dream journals, nature journals, bullet journals, commonplace books, or a combination of these concepts. Journaling causes you to reflect and expand and can be therapeutic to the highest degree. Write in your journal at the same time each day and journal in a way that feels right to you, keeping in mind it is for you and no one else.

WRITING POETRY

Writing poetry might not be a part of your regular leisure routine, but I believe every human should write a poem at least once in their lives. If you are more poetically inclined, you can make writing poetry a regular practice that, much like journaling, enriches your soul. It might feel daunting to stare at a blank page and write a poem, but work through the feelings of uncertainty and write from your heart. Choose the first topic that comes to mind that you feel excited about. Write without worrying whether it is good or not. Write a poem for someone or only for yourself. The act of creating will leave you feeling exhilarated.

WRITING LETTERS

Writing letters is a delightful novelty in our digital age. Surprise your friend or relative by writing them a letter. You can start with a postcard if a letter feels too daunting. At the beginning of reclaiming my letter-writing leisure time, I began by writing to one pen pal. This has slowly expanded to several friends that I write to across the world. We are sustained by our letters to each other; the exchange is a gift. Set up a writing desk that makes correspondence easy, with quality stationery, stamps, and pens. Keep the letters you receive in a beautiful box. Some might find it handy to compose letters on the computer in a digital file, and when you're ready to write back, simply transpose from the online document to your handwriting. Letter writing is a pastime that is not only relaxing but rewarding because it fosters connection without ever having to leave your home (that is, until you walk to the postbox).

GARDENING

Leave the phone inside, don your gardening gloves, go outside, and dig in the earth. Pull up weeds, trim your roses, or fertilize the flowers. While gardening, delight in the feeling of the fresh breeze on your skin, the sun on your back, and the earthworms you come across as you dig. Take note of the progress. You will find yourself so refreshed and relaxed when done and find yourself drawn into the private world you're creating out your window.

CRAFTS

Fiber arts like knitting or weaving, origami, textile crafts, embroidery, ceramics, and other crafty hobbies are an enriching activity for many people who love to unwind by working with their hands. Support your craft by being abundantly supplied and house your supplies in an easily accessible place. Set up a beautiful atmosphere to craft in, whether in your garden shed or a cozy, well-lit armchair. Listen to beautiful music, an audiobook, or just your own thoughts as you lose yourself in the mesmerizing act of creating. Create with no goal other than to experience heightened leisure. If you make something you want to gift to a friend or sell, that is an added benefit, but remember this leisure time is for you and your soul's growth.

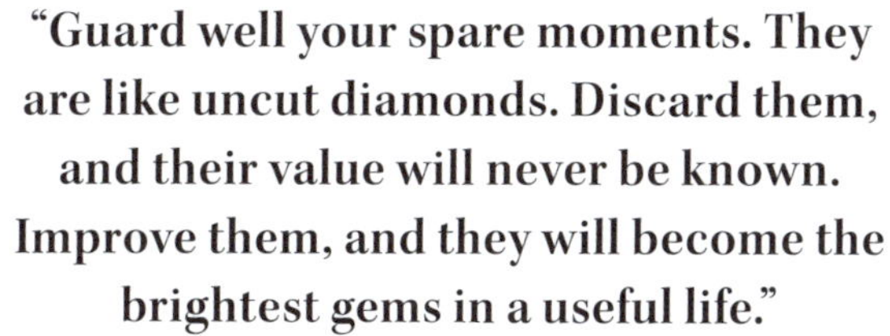

"Guard well your spare moments. They are like uncut diamonds. Discard them, and their value will never be known. Improve them, and they will become the brightest gems in a useful life."

—RALPH WALDO EMERSON

Tips on Implementing High-Quality Leisure:

Enjoy your activity at the same time each day. For example, play the piano every evening after dinner for 15 minutes.

Write it down on your to-do list or planner. By giving your hobby as much importance as your other daily tasks, you will take it more seriously.

Accept that the most productive thing you can do sometimes is to engage in high-quality leisure. If you have a mind geared toward productivity, you could be telling yourself the lie that you don't have time to rest in this way. But because high-quality leisure is so beneficial to our health, both mental and physical, we must realize that taking time for ourselves is the most productive way we can spend our time. My friend Dr. Chloe Carmichael, author of *Nervous Energy: Harness the Power of Your Anxiety*, presented this revelation to me.

Journaling Prompt:

Write down what you notice when you regularly start to implement your favorite pastimes back into your life. How is your health improving? Are you gaining mental clarity and feeling more rested?

Living Well on a Budget

The wonderful news about cultivating a satisfying life at home is that this path is often the friendliest on the wallet. When you spend time at home, you are more in control of the budget and unexpected costs are less likely. It can be shocking after going out to tally up the amount spent. Popping into shops, buying gas or train tickets, grabbing coffee, and stopping at a spot for lunch can truly add up. These ventures are fun and necessary every now and then, but if you find yourself on a budget, embrace the idea that you can still enjoy the experience of outings by recreating them at home.

Have you ever taken an outing that didn't go as planned? Maybe, you got stuck in a traffic jam, or the place you visited was so crowded you had to wait in long lines. Maybe, you spent a lot more money than you had set out to spend. We've all experienced disappointments with our outings only to return world-weary and be so thankful to finally be home. To save money, I try to capture the feeling of the adventure at home. Taking joy in simple pleasures at home can be so refreshing. I have compiled a list of simple pleasures that are satisfying to take part in at home. These activities can add beauty and joy to your life and are a welcome departure from your usual schedule. You'll likely not only save money but conserve your energy and rest through the experience. When you feel like you can't face going out, try one of these ideas instead:

AT-HOME CAFÉ

Recreate the coffee shop experience at home by making your favorite coffeehouse drinks. Invite friends to join you or go solo while reading a book in your favorite chair, just like a traditional experience. On the following pages are some at-home recipes to create delicious drinks. Each recipe serves one person, but you can easily double them to serve a guest. You will find these drinks so delicious and a fraction of the cost of your favorite coffeehouse beverage.

Iced Latte

Makes 1 serving

Coffee connoisseurs might be horrified that this recipe includes instant coffee; however, this portion of the book is discussing budgeting, and instant coffee is a very budget-friendly option. If you have a fancy espresso machine, I encourage you to use it instead. But if you find yourself without one, you'll be surprised how delicious and easy it is to use instant coffee for iced drinks. As another side note: I do not add sweetener to my coffee, but if desired, you can add your favorite syrup to taste.

1 teaspoon high-quality instant coffee
3 tablespoons hot water
¾ cup cold milk of choice
Ice

Mix instant coffee granules with the hot water until fully dissolved. Pour the cold milk on top and, blend using an immersion blender. Pour over ice in a tall glass. Enjoy with a straw.

Notes

London Fog Tea Latte

Makes 1 serving

This delicately flavored latte is so satisfying on a chilly autumn day, or serve it iced in the late spring for an elegant pick-me-up.

1 bag Earl Grey tea
½ cup boiling water
½ cup hot milk of choice
1 teaspoon honey or maple syrup
Dash of vanilla extract
Edible lavender buds, for garnish

Place the tea bag in the hot water and allow to steep for 3 to 5 minutes. Remove and discard tea bag. Stir in hot milk of choice, honey or syrup, and vanilla extract. Mix with a drink frother until foamy on top. Sprinkle with lavender buds.

Notes

Matcha Latte

Makes 1 serving

My favorite additions to use with matcha are almond milk and oat milk but you can experiment and find your own favorites, too.

1½ teaspoons high-quality matcha powder
1 tablespoon hot water
¾ cup hot almond milk
1 teaspoon honey or maple syrup (optional)

Sift the matcha powder into a cup. Add 1 tablespoon hot water. Whisk together with a hand whisk or milk frother until all the lumps are dissolved. Add the hot milk and sweetener and continue to blend until frothy. (If making an iced matcha latte, add cold almond milk instead of hot.)

Notes

Pistachio Rose Hip Latte

Makes 1 serving

This delightful tea latte has delicate flavors that are so complementary. If you cannot find pistachio milk, then try macadamia, hemp, coconut milk, or almond milk. If you don't have rose hip tea, hibiscus or rooibos tea work just as well.

1 cup pistachio milk
1 tablespoon honey (optional)
1 bag rose hip herbal tea

In a saucepan over low heat, heat the pistachio milk until hot but not boiling. Add honey, if desired. Whisk to incorporate the honey. Add the tea bag and cover. Let steep for at least 5 minutes. Pour into your favorite teacup.

Notes

READING NOOK

If the local library is crowded and you want some privacy, create a cozy reading nook where you can enjoy your books privately and in style. When I was a child, my grandmother's beachside house in Cambria, California, had two window nooks that converted to beds. Not only did I love sleeping in these nooks when I came to visit, but they also doubled as the most amazing reading spots. If you have a window with a great view and are able to add a bench or convert it to a window nook, this is a wonderful place to get lost in a book. Otherwise, a comfy armchair with a reading light, which is tucked away in a cozy corner, will do the trick.

AT-HOME RESTAURANT

If the budget is tight or you simply don't feel like leaving home but still desire the experience of your favorite restaurant, consider recreating it at home. Take your favorite dish from the menu and try to duplicate it. Light the candles, play the type of music the restaurant is known for, set the table, and experience an adventure at home for a fraction of the price.

MOVIE NIGHT

Freshly made popcorn dripping with hot butter, a hot chocolate brimming with whipped cream, your favorite people, and a good movie—what could be better? Turn off the lights, get comfy, and indulge in an optimal movie experience from your living room. With streaming options, enjoying a movie at home (for a fraction of the price of going to the theater) is now more accessible than ever. My family and I like to select a monthly movie night theme where, each Friday, we watch a film in line with the theme.

Some examples are:

Alfred Hitchcock Films—Scream at *The Birds*, become a voyeur in *Rear Window*, and learn how *To Catch a Thief*, while also versing yourself in classic cinema.

Anime Movies—Get lost in the wonderful and whimsical world of Studio Ghibli films like *Kiki's Delivery Service*, *Howl's Moving Castle*, and *Spirited Away*.

Jane Austen Cinema—Two words: Mister Darcy. Need I say more? Enjoy cinematic adaptations of *Pride & Prejudice*, *Emma*, and *Sense and Sensibility*.

Disney Favorites—Don't overlook old classics, like *Snow White* and *Cinderella*, or newer Disney features. The Disney theme never gets old, no matter how old you are!

Classic Children's Books on Film—From *The Secret Garden* and *Alice in Wonderland* to *Little Women*, revel in modern adaptations of your favorite childhood reads.

Mystery Night—Starting with *Clue* and ending at *Murder on the Orient Express*, consult your inner detective by watching one confounding mystery each week and enjoy figuring out "whodunit" with your loved ones.

Homemade Popcorn

Makes 4 servings

3 tablespoons oil
⅓ cup popcorn kernels
3 tablespoons melted butter (or to taste)
Salt, to taste

Heat oil in a large pan on medium heat. Pour in the popcorn kernels. Cover the pan. Cook on medium heat until the popping sound slows significantly. Turn off heat. Carefully open the lid. Pour melted butter on top and add salt. Mix.

GRACIOUS CRAFTS

Whether you consider yourself crafty or not (I actually don't consider myself very crafty), creating art with your hands is so therapeutic and satisfying. The following are easy crafts that anyone can do and that are best enjoyed at home.

PRESSING FLOWERS

Whether at the height of your garden's glory or the tail end of the blooms for the year, gathering flowers to press is a wonderful pastime. Relish the experience of selecting which flowers and foliage you'd like to preserve. Search for unusual flowers to press: often the ones that are too small or delicate for a bouquet work well here. If a beautiful rose has collapsed with age, you can collect the petals to press. Gather the amount you desire, all the while soaking in the garden. Even if you don't have a lot of flowers, you can still enjoy this activity with leaves alone. Sometimes, even weeds can make charming specimens, too. When you search in earnest, you can always find something pretty to capture. Once your flowers are gathered, arrange them in a flower press and press them according to the instructions. The pressing of flowers can take days in a traditional press or can take just a few minutes in a microwave press. Once pressed, there are so many crafts you can do with your pressed flowers. Here are some ideas:

Pressed Flower Bookmarks

You will need:

Glue
Pressed flowers
Cardboard bookmarks
Laminator sleeves
Laminator
Hole punch
Tassels

Glue pressed flowers on your bookmark front and back in a design that is pleasing to the eye. Allow the glue to dry. Place bookmarks in a laminator sleeve and run through a laminator on the hot setting. Cut out the bookmark leaving a small margin of laminated space. Punch a hole in the top of the bookmark. Thread a tassel through.

Pressed Flower Cards

You will need:

Pressed flowers
Cardstock cards
Glue

Arrange the pressed flowers in an attractive arrangement on the front of the cardstock. Glue in place. Dry.

Nature Journaling

You will need:

Journal
Glue
Pressed flowers
Pen or colored pencils

In your nature journal, glue the pressed flowers, only a few to each page, leaving yourself room to write. You can research the flower name and try to draw it, write how the flower makes you feel, or create a story or poem about the flower. If you create an entire book of these, this would make a meaningful gift for a child or dear friend.

Pressed Flower Wrapping Paper

You will need:

Recycled kraft paper
Scissors
Tape
Pressed Flowers
Glue
Twine or ribbon of choice

Pressed flowers are an enchanting way to personalize gift wrap. Wrap the gift with recycled kraft paper or desired wrapping, using scissors to cut paper to size and tape to secure the wrap. Then, glue the pressed flowers onto the most optimal areas to bring out the gift's charm. Let dry. Tie with twine or your favorite ribbon. Another idea is to write the name of the flower in pretty handwriting next to each flower. The recipient will appreciate the wrapping as much as the gift itself.

Pressed Flower Salt Dough Ornaments

You will need:

Salt Dough Ornaments (recipe follows)
Mod Podge
Small paintbrush
Pressed flowers
Twine or ribbon

Brush your fully cooked salt dough ornaments with a thin layer of Mod Podge, using a paintbrush. Arrange your pressed flowers any way you please. Brush another thin layer of Mod Podge on top of the flowers. When dry, thread a piece of twine or your favorite ribbon through the hole on top of the ornament for hanging.

Salt Dough

2 cups all-purpose flour
1 cup salt
1 cup water

Preheat the oven to 250°F. Combine flour and salt in a bowl. Gradually add 1 cup water, a bit at a time, until it is of a soft clay consistency. Place in the bowl of a stand mixer and set on knead setting or knead by hand for 7 to 10 minutes. Roll out the dough on a floured work surface. Use cookie cutters to cut into your desired shapes. Using a straw, cut a hole in the top of the salt dough ornaments. Bake for 2 hours or until dry. Allow to cool completely before decorating.

Homemade Lavender Bags

2 cups uncooked rice
1 cup dried lavender buds
7 to 10 drops lavender essential oil
Jute bags
Ribbon

In a bowl, combine the rice, lavender, and essential oil. Pour into jute bags and tie with a pretty ribbon. Keep these bags in your linen closet and drawers for a naturally beautiful scent and to repel moths.

Lavender Room Mist

¼ cup witch hazel
1 cup distilled water
25 to 30 drops lavender essential oil

Using a pouring funnel, pour the witch hazel and distilled water into a spray bottle. Then add drops of essential oil. Shake and spray when a fresh room scent is desired. It's great to keep this spray in bathrooms, too.

The Delightful Comfort of Home

As I write this, the past weekend was spent in Santa Barbara, California, at a rental vacation home. The rental was perfectly adequate with enough sleeping spaces and all the amenities one needs, but even so, staying at these rental homes highlights the importance of your own home comforts. It makes you think about how even the smallest details, like mattress firmness, pillow support, water pressure, towel fluffiness, functioning coffee machine with the right coffee, (I could go on, but I'll stop there) are so important. All these little details come together to make a home comfortable, and even though we had riotous fun (the kids were sad to leave), we were all thrilled to be back in our own beds when the trip was over. Everything in our homes is the result of a choice. We choose the mattress, pillows, towels, coffee maker. We set the water pressure and heater. We arrange everything according to our comfort, and rightfully so. All these minute decisions combine to make our home so delightful to come back to. Going away for a quick holiday makes you appreciate your own home like nothing else.

Choose to live a beautiful life at home, through your dress, your actions, and your decorating. Make your homelife so delightful that most experiences staying anywhere else pale in comparison. Your home will always be an ongoing project—not like a construction zone that is never finished but more like a delightful art project that you slowly add to over time. The more present you are living in your home, the more you can tweak problem areas of your life and transform them into triumphs. You will find yourself thriving in your space.

Notes

PART III: INSPIRATION

Inspirational Homes 

"A nation's culture resides in the hearts and the soul of its people."
—MAHATMA GANDHI

When curating an ideal life at home, it is helpful to consider pleasant past experiences and bring them to your current homelife. For example, if you stayed in a beautiful hotel and felt rested, luxurious, and completely at home, ask yourself what about your stay made you feel this way. If you were a guest in someone else's home and admired the way they lived or if you visited a country and felt smitten with one of their traditions, incorporate those aspects as much as you can into your own homelife. This will require adaptation. If you were staying at a chic hotel in Paris, for example, but you live on a farm in the Midwest, you'll need to adapt the living concept to fit your current life. The best way to do this is to think of why you felt so happy in your memory and then reflect about how you can incorporate it into your life. Journal about it.

In this chapter, I will share my own stories deriving inspiration from homes, hotels, and a few countries I have visited and how I have taken poignant aspects from those experiences to enrich my life at home.

MADAME CHIC'S PARISIAN APARTMENT

I have written a book series on the lessons I learned while living with Madame Chic and her family in the 16th arrondissement of Paris. The Chics' apartment was a source of great inspiration for me. The way they lived influenced my adulthood in ways that I could never have imagined. I recommend reading *Lessons from Madame Chic*, *At Home with Madame Chic*, and *Polish Your Poise with Madame Chic* for more inspiration.

MY CHILDHOOD HOME

My childhood home was a small three-bedroom house in the quiet suburbs of Los Angeles. It was a cookie-cutter home that was not fancy in any way, but we put our stamp on it as a family, and I loved living there. My mother is an excellent gardener, and our garden would stop neighbors in their tracks. She tended to her plants for hours and was often caught up in discussions with passersby on how she maintained such a lush paradise. She grew irises, roses, hydrangeas, daffodils, foxgloves, and so many other beautiful flowers, making the garden a magical place for me to explore. I spent so much of my childhood outdoors: helping my mom plant bulbs; climbing trees; reading in the grass with my dog, Goldie, as my pillow; and making fairy furniture out of twigs and grapevines with my dad.

While the outside of our home was framed by my mother's lush garden, the inside was characterized by my dad's love of literature and music. Books were everywhere, spilling out of his home office and lying around on coffee tables and end tables. Seeing my dad read so much definitely contributed to my own love of reading, and from the earliest age I can remember, I was always immersed in a favorite book series, taking my literary treasures with me all around the house.

Music played in our home nearly every day, too. Classical music poured from the stereo filling our four walls. Mozart, Bach, Chopin, and Beethoven became the soundtrack to our lives and contributed to my love of the genre as well as my desire to play the piano myself. My parents also listened to rock music by The Rolling Stones, The Mamas and the Papas, and Simon & Garfunkel. They also encouraged and appreciated the popular music my sister and I listened to from the time. The latest track from Dave Matthews Band or The Smashing Pumpkins would be played and listened to by our parents, which made us feel heard.

When I think back to my childhood, I realize what a major role our individual hobbies and passions played in creating a fulfilling life at home. Home is absolutely the place to draw out these interests no matter how eccentric they may be. My mother's gardening hobby and my dad's passion for music and reading are good examples of how one's personal interests can heighten life at home. Do you love books? Let them spill out of the bookshelves! Do you have a passion for gardening? Get planting to create the cottage garden of your dreams! Do you love music? Let your favorite pieces resound within your four walls. Home is made up of your collective interests. Your unique passions will season your homelife with individuality and wonder.

THE TUDOR MANSION

When I was growing up, my mother went back to school to get a degree in gerontology. While she was getting her degree, she worked part time as a girl Friday for a wealthy family in a nearby neighborhood. During the summer months when I was off school, I would sometimes accompany her to the house while she worked. From my adolescent point of view, it was less a house and more like a gigantic dollhouse-mansion paradise come to life. (In adult-speak, it would be called a Tudor-style home.) It was the grandest house I had ever stepped foot in,

and I always jumped at the opportunity to go with my mother to work. We would be there for several hours, and I always went off on my own to explore. Looking back, the family was incredibly gracious to allow a 10-year-old girl to walk around their mansion, lording about, as if I owned the place.

Every room in the house was lavishly decorated. This was in the late '80s to early '90s era when nostalgic décor was very popular, and the house had an opulent Victorian feel to it. In addition to all the typical rooms and areas you would expect in a house, there was also a conservatory, library, swimming pool, rose garden, formal living room, billiard room, playroom, west wing, and an east wing. I would sit in each room, take in its energy, and pretend I was the lady of the house. I decided "this was the life" and hoped and prayed I could live in a similar home one day. Upon reflection of my time in this Tudor mansion, I pinpointed key reasons why I felt so inspired in the space: the home was beautifully appointed, great to-dos were made for elevated leisure, and I felt opulent just for being there. Let's look at each of these points further.

Not only was the mansion beautifully decorated with tasteful furnishings and décor, but each room felt like it was complete. In my experience, so many homes are works in progress but rarely finished. You could walk into any room in this magical home and know it had been thoughtfully designed and decorated with purpose. The sense of completeness that comes with this gave me permission to rest in the space knowing I was amid beauty and intentional design. I realized this is the same feeling one gets when visiting a beautiful hotel. When sitting in a grand hotel lobby, it is not a "work in progress," and there is no indecisiveness to the design. The lobby displays a definite style and point of view. Likely a highly skilled interior designer worked with a talented crew to bring about an immersive experience with everything thoughtfully executed from the lighting to the armchairs to the plants. When sitting in this type of hotel lobby, you can simply enjoy what is and appreciate the point of view it expresses. That was the feeling I got in this Tudor home. There was a definite stylistic point that unapologetically gripped you. The only thing you could do was enjoy it. When I think of my own home this way, it helps me to make solid decorating and design decisions. I feel empowered to express my true style through my décor without compromising with wishy-washy choices. When I think back to how the style of this Tudor mansion encouraged me to visit it, I feel that much of my inspiration came from this place.

Regarding elevated leisure: the extra rooms designated for specific activities (billiard room, library, etc.) made me feel like I was a character in the board game Clue (without the murder). The feeling of leisure was exalted in this house. If you wanted to read a book, it was so luxurious to have an entire library where you could devote an hour to doing so. If you wanted to partake in the pursuits of growing orchids and indoor herbs, a trip to the conservatory was in order. If you wanted some recreation, including playing a game of pool or billiards, why head on into the billiards room, of course! While having these extra rooms is not a reality for most people, we can take away the higher idea behind these spaces and assimilate them into our own abodes. We should recognize that home is a place for pleasurable pursuits and that space can be made to prioritize their importance no matter how small your home is.

For example, our family loves playing chess and backgammon. We don't have a designated game room, but our formal living room houses these board games comfortably, and we are always ready for an impromptu round (or five!). In fact, our formal living room doubles and triples as a game room and music room since this is where our piano is. You can make your rooms multifunctional, according to your family's desires, with a little forethought and planning. We don't have a conservatory for growing plants, but I have taken my love of orchids all around the house, with the heaviest concentration of them in our primary bathroom and kitchen. Sure, they are not housed in greenhouse walls and ceiling of a conservatory or sunroom, but these spaces are ideal for growing and regrowing these exotic beauties. While I would love to have a home library one day, I make amends by creating several cozy spots around the house to curl up and read a good book. These spots are well-lit with comfortable chairs and tables or pedestals to hold a cup of tea and any accompanying items. Perhaps, one day I will build my own Tudor mansion, but in the meantime, I can recreate the feel of this custom home in my current space.

And, finally, the feeling of opulence I got from being in this Tudor house was the most intangible yet valuable takeaway. As soon as we drove into the circular driveway in our old Toyota station wagon, I felt like a queen coming home to her palace.

Instinctively, as a child, I soaked in the luxurious atmosphere by appreciating this lavishly appointed home and visualizing myself living in a space like that one day. I'd dress up on purpose when I knew I would be visiting because I wanted to match the surroundings by looking elegant. When we returned home after my mom's work was finished, I did my best to carry the feeling of opulence I cultivated to our house. I wanted to capture as much of the magic as I could from my time there, and in turn, I took better care of my room by keeping it clean and organized. Being in these elevated surroundings was not about the wealth that surrounded me while there but more about the feeling I got from being in that beautiful atmosphere. Even as a child, I had the instinct to "cut and paste" those luxuriant feelings from the Tudor mansion to my feelings at home. Ever since that formative experience as a child, I have tried to capture that feeling of luxury with me wherever I am. Sometimes, the feeling is more elusive than at other times, but I'll never forget the way that elegant Tudor mansion shaped me.

THE COASTAL COTTAGE

My grandmother always longed to live in Cambria, a picturesque seaside town in Central California. A creature of habit and familiarity, my grandfather did not want to leave their home in Fresno, California. She honored his wishes and stayed in Fresno. It was only after he passed away that my grandmother made the decision to sell the family home and move by the sea. After renting a few cottages there, she bought a little home in Cambria, right by the Cambria Pines Lodge. It was a modest space, but it was her complete heaven. She set it up for comfort and lived a very social life, staying active in the community and taking advantage of the shops, restaurants, and beautiful seascape as much as she could. Visiting her at this home as a teenager and young adult always felt like a welcomed exhale. I would get so excited at the end of our four-hour drive from Southern California to spot the rolling hills with grazing cows, thick forest trees, and ocean off in the distance. Grandma always made us feel at home and made sure we were comfortable.

Californian Olallieberry Pie

Of course, the spoiled antics of the grandmother/grandchild relationship accompanied my stay. Did I want olallieberry pie for breakfast? No problem! Did I want to take a bubble bath in her jet spa? Done! Did I want to sleep in and walk to the shops the next day? Penciled in! Grandma would give us what she called "mad money" to spend on whatever we liked. It was only $20, but that $20 made me feel rich because I could buy with it whatever I wanted. I would usually go to the local shops and buy soaps, lotions, lip balms, and other items teenagers desire. While my grandmother's modest home was nowhere near as fancy as the Tudor mansion, the feeling of rest and play I got from Grandma's house was even more nourishing and life-giving. I transfer these feelings to my life today in several ways. For example, if we have leftover pie after a holiday, I do not hesitate to eat it for breakfast the next day in Grandma's honor. I also try to consciously rest and collect that slightly naughty feeling of playing "hooky" that I had while there. I could read a book all day long, saunter to the table at mealtimes, go on nature walks with my cousins, and stay up late into the evening laughing. This was a home for recharging. I want that energy in my current home as well and don't want to have to wait until I am a grandma to achieve it.

I find that recreating the feeling from Grandma's house is about permission. One of the things my grandma was good at was giving "permission" to rest, live, and be joyful. She lived well into her 90s with this philosophy, and while it sometimes got her into trouble, it was also one of her most endearing traits. As I rushed through my busy days as a wife and mother of four young kids, I found myself not giving myself permission for much of anything except for work, serving, and more work. I would stay up late editing videos, get up early to write, and then cram in whatever I could throughout the day as I also homeschooled, cleaned the house, and looked after my family. The familiar saying "all work and no play makes Jack a dull boy" was indeed what I was unintentionally living. Except, for me, it was more like "all work and no play made Jennifer a stressed-out and frazzled woman." It was only after nearly a decade of this unsustainable lifestyle that I remembered my grandmother and her words of wisdom. I longed for the feeling of deep rest and joy I found at her house as a child. It's curious that, when I thought of her, I also thought of her home. The two were inseparable. And even when she finally moved into an assisted-living facility in Palm Springs, California, I still associated her with her coastal cottage. It was a place I didn't soon want to forget—a place that encouraged rest and gave one permission to put away all cares and eat olallieberry pie and ice cream for breakfast. Forget about healthy protocols or weight scales, we were having dessert first thing in the morning! In my home, I am passionately committed to creating a place that gives permission to go topsy-turvy every now and then and allow for deep unexpected pleasure.

Here are some ways I incorporate my grandmother's playful attitude into my life at home:

Enjoy dessert every day. Pie for breakfast is rare for me these days (though not off the table) but dessert everyday isn't. I have teatime every afternoon. The break from my hectic schedule is so welcome. I savor the hot sips of high-quality tea along with a crave-worthy dessert.

Throw out the to-do list every now and then. I usually am big on sticking to my plan for the day, but every now and then, I like to close my planner and forget my responsibilities. The kids and I will go on an adventure walk instead or watch a movie in the late afternoon. I tell myself my to-do list will still be there tomorrow.

Take an evening bath. I used to love the water jets in my grandmother's tub. And the fireplace at the foot of her bathtub made it so cozy to soak and think while watching the dancing flames. I don't have a fireplace in my current bathroom, but sometimes, I'll take a bath while it's still light outside so I can gaze out the window. I love watching the trees dance in the wind and the birds flying by. I'll see the occasional butterfly and dragonfly, too. It's a meditation on nature while soaking in delightful bath oils or salts. I always feel refreshed afterwards.

Go on long walks in the neighborhood. Stepping outside Grandma's door brought me straight into the woods, which I don't have in my own home, but I do feel the same sense of adventure when I embark on a walk in my neighborhood. I like to focus on the beautiful landscaping in my neighborhood while taking in the fresh air. I'll often notice the trees and how majestic they are.

THE TAOS PUEBLO

My aunt was married to a Native American man, and they lived on the pueblo in Taos, New Mexico. One of the most fun and memorable trips of my childhood was visiting them on the pueblo with my cousins. We were introduced to my new uncle's extended family and got to see firsthand the way of life on a Native American reservation. The pueblo houses were mostly

constructed of adobe. Their thick walls kept the interiors cool on the scorching hot summer days. The insides of the pueblos were sparsely decorated with only the bare necessities while also displaying important Native American art pieces like richly woven textiles and clay sculptures. I wish I had paid more attention to the details as a child, but I was on a wild adventure with my cousins and was largely oblivious to the privilege I was privy to with this inside peek into their culture. Looking back on the trip, I do remember their strong sense of cultural pride and fierce protection of traditions that seemed to bloom with everything they did. The Native Americans held their rituals and traditions passed on from generations past in venerable love. This infused their lives through the way they constructed and decorated their homes and through the observances of meaningful rituals and ceremonies. They generously shared them with outsiders like us.

Blue Corn Mush

Makes 2 to 4 servings

In New Mexico, we ate hot blue corn cereal in the mornings, which has a similar consistency to Cream of Wheat. Blue corn has many health benefits, including increased protein and antioxidants, and is packed with potassium and calcium.

3 cups water
¼ teaspoon salt
1 cup blue cornmeal

Bring 3 cups water and salt to a boil in a medium saucepan over medium-high heat. Turn heat to medium-low. Add blue cornmeal and stir until fully combined and creamy, 3 to 4 minutes. Serve with desired sweeteners, milk, and toppings.

THE WOODLAND RETREAT

In my early 20s, I was part of a theatre group that had me touring as a solo artist at colleges across the country. The job itself required me to work and travel alone, but each summer, our organization got together in the forest of Northern California to gather for a retreat. This trip was one of the highlights of my year. It was so fun to connect with my friends and colleagues out in nature. The retreat center we frequented was not fancy at all—think log cabins, bunk beds, and shared bathroom facilities—but the feeling behind the retreat was one of abundance and rest. Each meal would be taken in the dining hall, a room with several long tables that were amenable to conversation. The food would be displayed buffet-style on the long sideboard, where we had a selection of one or two meals made from organic ingredients. The drinks on offer were housed in large dispensers: plain water, citrus water, and herbal iced tea. The meals were nourishing and healthful, and the mealtime was well-organized, allowing us all to comfortably dine while enjoying each other's company. After each meal, we would walk in the forest, and several times a day, we met for group activities. I think back to this humble retreat center often, and while the style and aesthetic of my own home is very different, I love to capture that relaxed feeling of rest and nourishment I received during my stays there.

One of the key components to this feeling was the element of nature and how it played a part of our days on the retreat. Outside the door to my cabin, the forest vegetation greeted me: Douglas firs, redwood trees, Jeffrey and ponderosa pines, elderberry plants, and wild roses. The feeling of stillness and being away from big city life saturated the air with peace. While my current home is in a suburban setting, rather than an enchanting forest, I can bring the outdoors in as much as possible to create a similar feeling. I love to open the windows allowing the fresh air to purify the home, to cut fresh flowers and herbs and display them on our tables and nightstands, and to cook with what we grow. Bringing in the outdoors breathes life and energy into our home's interior and is the fastest way to energize a stale space.

Upon further reflection, I realized that the relaxed feeling I got at this retreat came from the simplicity of everyday life. For example, the menu was not extensive. There were usually two options: a main dish and a vegan alternative. You simply accepted what was there and were not distracted by an abundance of choice. The options of herbal iced tea or water demonstrated the same concept. We were happy with what was offered and accepted it with gratitude. Sometimes, when I go to a restaurant and the menu is large, I will select my dish and wonder while I'm eating it if a different choice would have been better. When the choices are narrowed and I accept what is, I can enjoy my choice fully. Eliminating choice and narrowing in on what I want is a great way to simplify my life at home. I can create easy weekly menus for my family and be happy with them. I can declutter my closet and be okay with keeping less, releasing the need to hold on to things "just in case." Simplifying and accepting "what is" can be very freeing and relaxing.

A final reason why the retreat left such a big impression on me was the elimination of distractions. There was no technology on this trip. There were no blaring televisions; we didn't have our laptops with us, and cell service was bad, so we barely used our phones. This required a conscious connection with everyone around us, embracing stillness through a quieter existence, and picking up some of the lost arts of leisure, such as playing board games, having conversations in rocking chairs, and taking nature strolls. While it is not realistic to banish technology from our lives at home, we can recreate the retreat feeling at home by consciously disconnecting from technology at regular intervals: putting the laptop away by 4:30 p.m., for example, dedicating a set time to watch television, and purposely leaving your phone in the other room to avoid checking it. Working through the withdrawals you feel from being connected to your devices can help you retreat deeper into the presence of family life at home. You can become in tune with the rhythms of the day and happier for being disconnected from the tethers of online life.

THE ENGLISH COUNTRY HOME

When visiting my in-laws for the first time in England, I was highly out of my comfort zone. Our driver pulled into the private gates of their stately English country home. The walk to the front door was flanked by moss-covered lion statues that revealed an imposing brick house covered with climbing ivy. Newly married and desperately wanting to make a good impression with my in-laws, I tried my best to look presentable. I immediately took my shoes off at the door. I figured it was the polite thing to do as I usually took off my shoes before entering most homes in America, but I noticed a bit too late that I was the only one to do this. I found myself barefoot, walking around their stately house while everyone else was well-shod. Oh dear, this wasn't going as well as I'd hoped! As I'm writing this book, 19 years later, I have become much more comfortable in this English country house that I've gotten to know so well over the years and can smile at the timid young lady so many years ago who trembled at the sight of the imposing home and the people in it. My in-laws' beautiful home in Surrey has remained a design inspiration to me ever since. My mother-in-law has a talent for interior design, and each room is decorated with deliberate chic. She decorates with tromp l'oeil wall murals, cozy textiles, neutral furniture, and lots of antiques to create an eclectically eccentric feeling of country opulence.

My favorite part about their home is the gardens, which keep rhythm with the seasons in a way that stays with your soul. The pool is surrounded by rambling climbing white roses that burst into bloom for about two months a year. The deep pink and fragrant Gertrude Jekyll rose trees form circles around lavender and multicolored roses that could be the

feature at the Chelsea Flower Show. The field in the back was recently rewilded, and I have spent many magical afternoons wandering the paths as I am flanked by tall grasses, blue dragonflies, and ladybugs. I cherish making sprawling bouquets to show off the abundance of flowers whenever I am there, and the English love of roses certainly follows me back home to California as I cultivate my own rose gardens in my home's front yard and backyard.

My in-laws' home is a great example of decorating on theme. Their home is an English manor in the countryside and is decorated as such. If you have ever been in a home that was decorated contrary to the home's style, you've likely felt a disconnect between home and design. I have walked into a Victorian house, for example, that was gutted to have a modern interior. Something felt very "off" about being in this space. My in-laws' home embraced the English country aesthetic and unapologetically embodied it in every room with personal touches and traditional décor.

A final inspiration I have taken from this space is my mother-in-law's attention to detail. Every room was curated. If there was clutter on top of any surface, it wouldn't last long. She has a way of arranging everything to look aesthetically pleasing and intentional. Coffee-table books are stacked just so, and picture frames and decorative objects are always arranged for maximum beauty. I think of her when styling my surfaces with an eye for aesthetics always at the forefront of my mind.

Journaling Prompt:

What are the top inspirational homes in your life? Think back to your childhood. Were there any homes that made a deep impression on you? As an adult, what experiences have you cherished that inspire you to live well at home? Expand your options to not only homes of friends and family members, but also hotels or vacation properties you visited. How did these places make you feel? What is at the heart of their inspiration for you? How can you incorporate this inspiration into your life at home now?

International Inspiration

The best part about traveling is choosing the most meaningful experiences from your trip and incorporating them into your life at home. If you have read my Madame Chic series, you know that living in Paris in my early 20s completely transformed my life. I brought back so many French traditions I learned during my time there and adapted them to my life in America that I was able to fill three volumes of books with the lessons I learned. But France is not the only country that has inspired my living. In all my travels, each country has taught me at least one thing (if not many) about living well at home. Here are takeaways from some of my other travels that I have incorporated into my life. As you read, I encourage you to think of how your travels have shaped your life in meaningful ways.

Ooh La La!

PANAMA

My mother is from Panama but moved to the United States when she was just 19 years old and has called California her home ever since. Even though I have only visited Panama once, when I was 13 years old, I brought back so many memories from my journey. As this was my first trip outside of the US, I vividly remember the intense heat I felt when disembarking from the plane. California was hot, but this feeling of deep heat near the equator was something I wasn't accustomed to. I immediately was taken by the lushness of the plants and wildlife. We were at the periphery of the jungle, and I was very aware of its presence. As we were driven from the airport to my grandmother's house, I'll never forget what I saw: a chicken running down the street with a snake in its mouth! That wasn't a sight I was used to seeing in California!

The people in Panama were open, warm, friendly, and sociable. Friends and family would walk with ease back and forth to each other's houses, stopping for long chats, sharing meals together, and laughing. I didn't speak Spanish, so I was not able to follow along with the conversations I heard. But I do remember eating heaps of delicious food: spaghetti with ultra-large meatballs and a well-seasoned sauce was one of my favorites. I also loved the fried plantains, rice, beans, salsas, and fried savory pastries, too, all washed down with

Malta Vigor, a cream-like bitter soda that was such a treat for me.

When we went on walks in the jungle, I remember feeling scared of the wildness around me. The ants were so large! They carried leaves on their backs that made the ground appear to be a green conveyer belt. Panama presented life in full color. Not only was the lush landscape a deep, impenetrable green, but the buildings, clothing, and art were bright and buoyant. Wanting to bring a bit of this color back home, we visited with the Kuna women who make the famous Panamanian molas, handmade quilted textiles known for their vivid color palette. I bought crab and bird molas, and I have them proudly hanging in my home to this day. While I wish I had spent more time in Panama and hope to go back one day to explore my roots more, I think about my trip a lot and draw from much of my journey to enhance my homelife in California.

The main essence that impressed me with Panama was the deep sense of the wild. The jungle felt expansive, untamed, and awe-inspiring. No matter where you were, even if in the city center, you were aware of the jungle's presence—the untamed wilderness on the border of everything. I hold tendencies toward primness and properness. The wild has always fascinated me, but I seem to push away from it. Incorporating wild aspects into my life at home provides a much-needed balance for me to counteract my more rigid nature. I can bring aspects of the wild into my life through cooking. I love whipping up traditional recipes that my mother taught me like fried plantains, lentils, rich stews, and other nutrient-dense foods that she cooked for me as a child. I can spend more time in the garden, grounding into wild nature and appreciating the indigenous plants in my backyard. And while I don't climb trees like I did when I was a kid, I can certainly appreciate them and embrace them in my heart. My intentionality finds me marveling at the wildlife as well. I feed the birds each week and frequently commune with a wild rabbit that has grown comfortable with me. While I probably won't see a chicken running down the street with a snake in its mouth in California (let's hope not, anyway), I can take that sense of awe and reverence with me into the wild of my own home.

Another way I can incorporate the beauty of Panama into my life is through the easygoing nature of its people. Aunts and uncles, neighbors, and friends would stop by any time and be welcomed. There was such a relaxed feeling among the people amid high camaraderie. Most people have fantasies of easily and regularly entertaining family and friends in their homes. Watch any home improvement show, and the guests will likely talk about "entertaining." But how often do we entertain in our homes? Is it only on Thanksgiving, Christmas, and Easter? When we do entertain, it may feel more like a stressful chore than an enjoyable and relaxed event. The entire house needs to be cleaned. The menu must be meticulously planned, all the clutter banished, the right drinks and hors d'oeuvres served, and, oh dear, what does the powder room look like? Did anyone bother to clean it? In Panama, these things were never a concern. People would stop by each day unannounced and were welcomed with ease and happiness. The emphasis was less on impressing one's guests and more on enjoying their company. I can't imagine any guests popping over in Panama and secretly scoffing at the dust on the host's floorboards. Come to think of it, I don't think guests even do this in America! But we, as hosts, feel like everything needs to be perfect. How do we incorporate this with balance into our lives at home?

I like to keep the front rooms in the house "ready for company." This doesn't mean they are spotless showrooms that no one can go in until a guest stops by, but they don't have clutter, they have many comfortable seats and places to set a drink down, and they are attractively decorated and pleasant. If an unexpected guest drops by, we can comfortably sit in our front room, and even though it's not immaculate, my perfectionist tendences can embrace the Panamanian inspiration of treasuring my guest's company without worrying about toys scattered across the floor and dirty dishes in the sink. Living well in this way is about marrying your basic nature (wanting everything to be beautiful and perfect) with a healthy reality (realizing nothing is ever perfect so drop it already and relax). Embracing this, the next time I feel panicky about an unexpected guest, I can take a deep breath, embrace my social Panamanian nature, and simply say, ¿Qué xopá? (What's up?)

SPAIN

My husband's former business required us to travel to Spain once a year to visit the shoe factory in Alicante, a coastal city in the southeast region. I always looked forward to this trip, not only because Manuel, the factory owner, and his employees were so gracious, but also because this part of the world was beautiful. We'd stay in a hotel on the sea that had a circular window in the grand hallway with a perfect view of the ocean. On days off, I'd wander around the hotel with a book, laying in sun beds, and simply taking in the gorgeous view. I was a bit thrown off in the beginning when we would make dinner plans with Manuel and company, and they would tell us to meet them at 9:00. "You mean nine in the evening?" I asked my husband, incredulously. He only smiled at me and realized it was probably not wise to tell me what I was in for. We would meet our company at 9:00 p.m. and walk around the town. The evening was still warm, and people were spilling out of cafés, enjoying life, and socializing. I began to wonder when we would actually get to the eating part of the evening. (I am notorious for setting early dinner hours—at the latest 5:00 p.m.) We settled into the back room of a charming restaurant with local color and put in our order around 9:45 p.m. Yes, you read that correctly! The dinner wasn't served until after 10:00 p.m. I couldn't decide if I was so ravenous that I would scarf down the dinner like a wolf, or if I was beyond hunger and couldn't be bothered to eat. I needed to summon up my appetite, however, because an enormous pan of paella was brought before us all and ceremoniously dished out. Maybe, I just needed to relax. When in Spain, do as the Spaniards do and all that. After all, we can't all eat at 5:00 p.m. and go to bed with a cup of herbal tea. I decided to relax and enjoy the late dinners the entire trip. When reflecting on my Spanish adventures, I wondered how I could bring this essence of adventure into my life at home.

Traveling to other cultures where their habits are wildly different from your own is a life-expanding event. While I am never trading the "early bird special," I like occasional twilight dinners that go late into the evening and relaxing my rigidity every now and then. Being a creature of habit and routine can be a good thing (especially when implementing method and order), but sometimes, those habits need to be turned upside down in lieu of going with the flow. When I turned 40, I adopted intermittent fasting as a lifestyle, which means I don't eat anything after my early dinner. No snacking. I still adhere to this lifestyle because it gives me a healthy discipline, and I feel better than I ever have before. However, on movie nights with the kids, I can easily throw my usual eating routines out the window and indulge in hot chocolate and popcorn with melted butter. Or if we have a dinner party, I will be lingering at the table until 10:00 p.m. The key is being open enough to relax my strict schedule at home and realize that nothing bad will happen if I stray from it every now and then. I was so out of my comfort zone in Spain with the late-night meals. It was good for me to see an entire vibrant community of people that lived this way and thrived. Sure, it might not be ideal to digest a very rich meal as you're trying to go to sleep, so I wouldn't suggest this every night unless your body is used to it, but the social benefits from enjoying these late meals far outweighed any discomfort I had from shaking up my routine. I continue to invoke this experience in Spain to relax my routines at home.

ITALY

I was fortunate enough to tour parts of Italy in my college years. I visited Rome and Venice and hit up all the major spots any tourist could dream of. Apart from the awe and wonder of witnessing the ruins of ancient history and observing some of the most fashionable people on the planet, my favorite part of Italy, naturally, was the food. The flavorful pastas and pizzas will remain among my most-loved meals. The pastries and coffee, too! I was excited to return to Venice several years later with my husband. While there, I had a seemingly mundane mishap that has remained with me. A fan of presentable sleepwear, I bought a beautiful floral Calvin Klein nightgown for my Italian vacation. I draped it over the side chair in our charming Venetian hotel room. My husband and I went out to explore the town, marveling at the stationery shops, touring the cathedrals, and feeding the pigeons. When we got back to the hotel, our room had been made up by housekeeping. There was only one problem: I couldn't find my beautiful nightgown. When I left, it was draped on the chair. Now that I was back, I noticed it wasn't there. I looked in the closet, and it was not hung up either. I looked in my suitcase. Not there. Not in the bathroom. I searched through the drawers. Not there. It was nowhere to be found. I figured that when housekeeping changed the sheets, maybe, they accidentally picked it up, and it was now in the hotel laundry. This was a brand-new (pricey) nightgown, and I didn't want to lose it, so I called the reception desk. They said they'd look, but they didn't see it in the laundry. They even sent someone to come to the room to hunt for it. It was nowhere to be found. I didn't think anyone would have stolen it. What a random thing to steal! And nothing else was taken from the room. Perplexed, I got ready for bed that night with my spare pajamas. Thankfully, I brought two options! As I put my head on the pillow, I turned on my side and felt something under my head. It was my nightgown! Housekeeping had put my nightgown under the pillow. I remembered keeping my pajamas under my pillow as a child but had not considered this as a possibility when I couldn't find it in the hotel. In many cultures, tucking your pajamas behind your pillow is a normal daily routine. Pajamas can be worn two nights in a row, after all. My children now place their pajamas under their pillow if they plan to wear them the next evening. Not everything needs to be washed after only one wear, and my Italian adventure was a great reminder of this.

SRI LANKA

I was fortunate to stay in Sri Lanka with my college roommate and her family after graduation. What an eye-opening trip it was! I had never been in that part of Asia before, and I was amazed by the exotic beauty that surrounded me everywhere. The Sri Lankan people are friendly, kind, and so creative. My roommate's family home was opulent and stunning. There was no other way of putting it. It was grand on a scale that was intimidating to me. So much so that I didn't know how to voice my admiration to her. I shyly said nothing at all other than the odd, "wow!" and "thank you" every now and then. They had a household staff that were attentive to my needs, and I felt overwhelmed with gratitude for being able to stay there and experience their lovely way of life. My room was large and spacious with a sumptuously comfortable bed and a large bouquet of fresh flowers waiting for me. This was hospitality on another level. I enjoyed well-cooked meals with her family as well as outings at the finest restaurants around.

When I think back on this trip, it's funny what details come up in my mind so many years later. I vividly remember one of the breakfasts that was served to me. It was a thick spear of pineapple sliced like a filet mignon. The pineapple was served on beautiful china alongside a cup of sweet, creamy tea. I loved the simplicity of this breakfast. The sweetness of the pineapple was unparalleled. There were probably other breakfast items offered as well, but I remember that slice of pineapple and cup of tea so clearly. The pineapple was a mere slice of fruit but was presented beautifully and with majesty. It was a potent reminder that even the most common things in life can be made special with their presentation.

While there, we did some traveling around Sri Lanka, and in each hotel, we were greeted with a glass of fresh fruit juice and an abundance of hospitality. At one hotel, I remember sitting on the veranda with our juice and scouring the exotic and expansive view while our bags were being placed in our room. The pause before unpacking was most welcome. We slowly sipped our beverages and felt like royalty surveying our empire! This experience has reminded me to pause at home and take in the majesty of certain moments (like twilight) rather than rushing from point A to point B.

THAILAND

On the same Sri Lanka trip, my roommate's family arranged a journey to Thailand for us. I was awed by the beauty of its beaches and the magnitude of its temples. Thai food is a favorite of mine, so I couldn't get enough of the Pad Thai, Pad See Ew, and Thai curries. This is also where I (aptly) discovered Thai massage. Massages in the United States were pricey and a rare luxury for me during this time, and I was floored by how affordable the massages were in Thailand. My friend and I had several massages while there, and I thoroughly enjoyed each one, although on one occasion, my friend and I were next to each other in a large room with several open beds. The massage therapists were contorting our bodies into so many extreme positions that we caught glance of each other and burst into giggles that barely subsided until the massage was over. Not so relaxing, but the laughter was good for the soul. My body felt so good getting such regular massages; I made it a priority to get regular massages back home in America. I found a wonderful massage therapist who gave in-home massages. I indulge in this luxury twice a month. When I am not able to get a massage at home but need one, I do several stretching exercises that help tremendously with relaxation. One exercise, I do every day upon waking. It is a head and neck stretch:

> *Nod your head three times forward with your chin down and three times back with your chin up. Then, three times to the left side (with your ear going down toward your left shoulder) and three times to the right side. Then, roll your head three times to the left and three times to the right, all the while breathing deeply.*

Incorporating this morning stretch has helped me tremendously. I tend to store stress in my neck and shoulders, and this starts the day off right by stretching out that problematic area. I also repeat this stretch any time I feel stress throughout the day as a way to break up the tension. While I cannot get massages as frequently as I got them in Thailand, I can certainly channel the relaxation and joy I had there and treat my body accordingly at home.

PORTUGAL

My family and I spent several weeks in Portugal one autumn, staying at the picturesque seaside town of Vale de Lobo. My husband was with the older children, and I took the baby on a walk to the local grocery store because I needed a strong coffee. Even though I was enjoying my stay, I was traveling with a baby and was still sleep-deprived. Dreaming of a grande-sized or maybe venti-sized takeaway coffee from the little café, I walked down the hill with anticipation as I reached the grocery store. There was a gathering of people, mainly locals, at the coffee bar. I maneuvered the stroller into the room, and in very broken Portuguese, I ordered a large coffee "to go." The barista glanced at me inquisitively. I wasn't sure how to say "to go" in Portuguese, so I began miming myself drinking a large coffee and walking out the door. (In retrospect,

I blame this cringey behavior on my lack of sleep.) The barista nodded at me in what seemed like confused resignation, and as I waited for my coffee, I observed all the other patrons of the coffee shop. They were men and women, many in business suits, all drinking tiny espressos out of actual porcelain espresso cups. Hmmm. I wondered why they all ordered the same thing. And it was kind of cool that they stayed there and were talking to each other. How social! I was with a cranky baby and didn't speak the language, so it wasn't for me to stay, but I liked what I saw.

The barista motioned for my attention, and I happily went up to collect my coffee. He had poured an espresso into a little plastic cup. I wondered where my large coffee was. How was I supposed to pour cream into this? Maybe, I should have said "latte" instead of "café." But apart from the black espresso issue, I was concerned about the cup. I was pretty sure the cup was a water cup and not meant for hot coffee. That's when I realized that the barista was trying to appease my bizarre request for a takeaway coffee by pouring it into a water cup. It was clear that my very American version of coffee was not something that was offered here. They had espresso and that was about it. And one does not need to take espresso "to go."

I thanked him and took my flimsy cup of joe out the door, inwardly laughing as it splashed and sloshed over the sides of the thin, plastic cup as I navigated the stroller up the windy hill.

CAFÉ

This incident made me reevaluate my "to-go" mindset. Once upon a time in Paris, I embraced the slow-living café culture and reveled in sitting at cafés and people-watching while enjoying my drink. Several years back in America had me used to my drive-thru Starbucks orders happily sipped in the car or on the go. There's nothing wrong with this necessarily as these giant coffees have gotten me through many a hectic morning, but there was something jovial and enriching about seeing the Portuguese café patrons take a pause in their day to enjoy their espresso where they were. A few sips and it was gone, but the coffee was high-quality as was the company. I liked that. Venture into a café now, and most people are on their cell phones. They are not drinking out of porcelain mugs while having a chat with strangers. I remind myself of this at home when I am wont to make myself a coffee or tea and take it around the house with me while I do other things. Even though this might be the eventual outcome, I always begin with taking my first sips consciously. If it's tea, I serve it in a nice teacup and sit down to have it. I have a habit of pouring my first cup of coffee in my favorite cup (a Sherlock Holmes mug) and taking my first sips outside, weather permitting. The higher idea is to consume the drink in a conscious and meaningful way, not absentmindedly while doing other things. The next time I visit Portugal, I'll be sure to order my espresso "to stay."

FIJI

One of the most enjoyable and memorable trips of my life was my stay in Fiji when I was 23 years old. I met my cousin there, and together, we island-hopped for 10 days. My cousin is a world-class traveler, so I was happy to have her plan the details of the entire trip. Taking the speed boat to our first island had me experiencing a euphoric *Titanic* movie "I'm the king of the world" moment. The feeling of the hot sun on my skin and the rushing wind from the tiny boat—sailing on the most crystal-clear waters I had ever seen—had me stretching my arms out in sheer exhilaration. My cousin and I settled into our hut and were told by the accommodation staff that it was "time for tea." No words get me more excited than those, so we walked in great anticipation to the dining hut. There, we were given large colorful ceramic mugs. A lovely lady in a colorful caftan dress came around and poured steaming hot black tea into our mugs. There were little pots of milk flakes for us to stir into the tea, if we desired, and lumps of sugar, too. Then, we were served a thick slice of coconut cake. To say I felt like I was in heaven was an understatement. I was used to dainty and refined tea experiences with tiny bone china cups served with savory sandwiches and mini cakes. Don't get me wrong, I like that, too, but this was my first time experiencing such a relaxed teatime. The mugs, the milk flakes, and the generous slice of cake loosened me up a bit and had me bend my expectations. We were now on island time, and this was teatime, island-style.

Teatime in Fiji quickly became my favorite time of day. We were not staying in fancy resorts (we were on poor, graduate-student budgets), but leaving the comfort of our sun beds on the beach to sit on the long wooden benches to take tea with our fellow island hoppers felt like a priceless luxury. Whenever I'm feeling a bit too "stuffy" about teatime back at home, as if the sandwiches need to be a certain way and the setup needs to be perfect, I am reminded of those casual teas on the beach. They reminded me that no setting or experience is too casual to enjoy a cup of tea. Also, like the revelation I had with the Portuguese coffee, I noted the complete joy that teatime held when shared with others. While I typically take teatime alone at home, I will also often incorporate my family if they are available. We will go outside and sit by the pool with our tea and treats and relish the afternoon, island-style. Now, that is priceless.

ENGLAND

England is my second home. It's also the part of the world where I have spent the most time abroad. I am so familiar with it that, each year when we return, a pang of nostalgia and excitement permeates my being. I have taken so much living inspiration from this majestic country that it is hard to narrow down the meaningful ways it has impacted me at home, but I would say that the main way is through marrying tradition with eccentricity, whimsy, and literary wonder. In this sense, England abounds with inspiration. While there, I have seen hedgehogs, bumblebees, foxes, moles, and toads, which naturally remind me of my favorite characters from the Beatrix Potter and Sir Kenneth Grahame books. I've popped into pubs like The March Hare in Guildford that has subtle nods to *Alice in Wonderland* in its décor and ambience. I've dined in one of Agatha Christie's favorite pubs in Chelsea and visited Shakespeare's house and 221B Baker Street to boot! England's rich literary history can't help but make itself known to everyone who visits. I like to honor this rich literary heritage by surrounding my own home with my favorite books. You can find them displayed on bookshelves, bedside tables, coffee tables, and the fireplace mantel. I'll select certain fabrics because they remind me of *Alice in Wonderland*, or I'll even choose paint color because the name of the color is prominently

featured in a favorite Emily Dickinson poem (Alabaster). At Halloween, in a nod to Edgar Allan Poe, I'm more likely to put out a raven statue or two than skeletons. I value authors from all cultures, not just England, so the literary references found around my home reflect that (hence Dickinson and Poe, et al). But England reminds me that my love of literature can be reflected in my surroundings, and all the whimsy and nostalgia they bring are meant to be enjoyed.

JAPAN

At the time of writing this, I have traveled to the wonderful country of Japan on two separate occasions. Both times to do book tours and appear on a television show. While filming segments for the TV show, I was able to travel to Japanese homes and help people curate their own ten-item wardrobe and cultivate some of the beautiful living habits I wrote about in the Madame Chic series. While many of the people I helped on the show had the issue of too many clothes (one gentleman I helped had over 100 pairs of jeans!), some of them were able to teach me a thing or two about minimalism. For example, one home I toured had some Christmas decorations displayed on their mantel. When I entered, I took note of their beautiful and minimal decorations. They told me that they loved decorating for Christmas and got joy from their mantel decorations. Their delight in these subtle and minimal decorations made an impression on me. Back home, we go all out decorating for Christmas. Sometimes, I feel like every room in the house needs to contain holiday decorations. While it is certainly nice to decorate for the festive season, I was also inspired by the minimal decorations this family enjoyed. They derived great pleasure from seeing the few decorations on their mantelpiece and felt content with that. I remind myself of that when I feel the urge to go out and buy more and more to decorate my home. I have curated a beautiful collection of Christmas decorations over the decades that I happily display in all our main rooms of the house, but my eye is on quality not quantity. The Japanese family reminded me to be happy with what I have and not feel like I need more, more, more.

Another wonderful tip from my time in Japan that I employ every so often back in California is the savory breakfast. Before traveling to Japan, I had a very small list of acceptable foods that I would even consider for breakfast. But my first morning in Japan, while perusing the buffet at the hotel breakfast, I noticed a few unusual menu items: fish, rice, salad, miso soup, and other savory items were on display next to the typical American fare. Not feeling like pancakes, I decided to give the savory Japanese breakfast a try. Wow! Not only was it delicious first thing in the morning, but I felt great all day, too. I have since learned that when cultivating healthy glucose levels, a savory breakfast is recommended. I don't have a savory breakfast every day back home, but on days when I have leftovers from the night before, either fish or a savory stew, I will absolutely have it for breakfast, with a nod to my Japanese friends and their wise and healthy habits.

The Japanese art of presentation also left a deep impression on me. Other than France, I had never traveled to a country that took so much pride in the presentation of literally everything.

I went to a café to buy a tea drink (which, by the way, they totally make "to go") and a pastry and found them wrapping the pastry in the most intricate way as though it was a gift. This is not an anomaly. When I went shopping in little boutiques to buy presents for friends and family back home, the salespeople would wrap the items in beautiful wax paper and seal it with stickers. The precision of the wrapping was impressive, too. On my best day wrapping Christmas presents, I could not rival the exactness of this wrapping. The Japanese, along with the French, inspire me that everything can be presented beautifully, from my kids' birthday presents to the impromptu cake I bake on a rainy Saturday afternoon. Life is a gift, and what we make and give can also be presented like one.

Journaling Prompt:

What homes from your past have inspired you to live well? What memories stay with you and will never go away? What can you take from your travels to enrich your life at home today?

Conclusion

How you live at home is one of the most important aspects of your life to get right. Once you set yourself up for living well at home, you create a foundation for success, comfort, and security that is unparalleled. No matter what happens in the outside world, you can always return to your sacred place and know you will find comfort, a nourishing meal, and meaningful connections that will center you and bring equilibrium back to your days. If you have ever been dissatisfied with any aspect of running your home, you know how it can wreak havoc in your life. That's why not only getting functionality right but also taking it a few steps further to curate beauty and comfort fosters an environment for you to blossom and thrive. My hope is that this book will always stay with you to guide and encourage you to create the life you desire. May you find joy every day at home, and may that joy permeate everything you do and reach far beyond your front door to everywhere you go and to everyone you meet.

And remember, no matter what stage of the journey you are on: whether you're implementing cleaning routines, refining your leisure time, or hosting a dinner for 20 people, *enjoy the process.* The end result is not the goal. Daily Connoisseurs relish everyday life, and that includes all steps made towards the ideal. You are not behind. You are right where you need to be. Take pleasure in every moment, and while you're at it, remember to keep calm and remain classy, as we Daily Connoisseurs like to say.

Notes

Notes

Notes

Notes